IMAGES OF
FOOTBALL

IMAGES OF
FOOTBALL

TIM HILL

Photographs by the
Daily Mail

This is a Parragon Book
First published in 2005

Parragon
Queen Street House
4 Queen Street
Bath, BA1 IHE

All photographs © Associated Newspapers Ltd
Text © Parragon 2005

Produced by Atlantic Publishing

A catalogue record for this book is available
from the British Library.

ISBN 1-40544-891-1
Printed in China

Introduction

Association Football was born on 26 October 1863, when eleven clubs met at the Freemason's Tavern, Great Queen Street, London. The next two decades spawned the world's first cup and league competitions. The early years were faltering ones: the 1873 FA Cup final kicked off at 11 a.m. to avoid clashing with the Boat Race; and at the world's first official international fixture, between England and Scotland in 1872, the attendant photographer refused to record the event for fear of being unable to sell his pictures. His concerns were soon allayed: football became the people's game at home and spread to all corners of the globe. Lavishly illustrated with superb photographs from the archives of the *Daily Mail*, *Images Of Football* provides a fascinating pictorial record of football in England, the cradle of the Beautiful Game.

IMAGES OF
FOOTBALL

WALKER SPARES FA'S BLUSHES

Above: Aston Villa and Huddersfield Town fans in buoyant mood as they make their way to Stamford Bridge for the 1920 Cup Final. This was the first of three finals played at Chelsea's ground before Wembley Stadium was ready to host the annual showpiece. Villa won 1-0 after extra-time to lift the Cup for a record sixth time. In the semis two goals from Villa's Billy Walker had helped knock Chelsea out of the competition. It saved the FA from an embarrassing infringement of its own rules, which stated that the match had to be played at a neutral venue.

Opposite: Fans of The Wednesday and Everton pass St Paul's Cathedral on their way to the 1907 FA Cup Final, staged at Crystal Palace. Mid-table Wednesday – the club didn't incorporate the city's name until 1929 – upset the form book by beating title-chasing Everton 2-1. That season saw Woolwich Arsenal lead Division One briefly, the first southern team to top the table since the inauguration of the Football League in 1888-89. But the Gunners faded to finish seventh as Newcastle won the championship for the second time in three years, thus continuing the northern clubs' period of dominance.

MUST-SEE MATCHES

Left: Fans probably prepared themselves for an attritional Cup Final in 1912. Finalists Barnsley had put out Bradford City in the fourth round – but only after three goalless draws. In the semi-final against Swindon Town the Second Division side played out another 0-0 draw before winning the replay 1-0. The final pitted the Yorkshire club against First Division side West Bromwich Albion. It was another goalless affair, Barnsley's sixth in the competition overall. The replay at Bramall Lane looked as if it was heading the same way before Tufnell won the match for the Tykes in the dying seconds of extra-time. After three successive drawn finals, the FA ruled that in future extra-time would be played in the first match.

Opposite: There is a long history of fans pouring into grounds – not always by the conventional access points – and finding the best vantage points from which to view matches. Tens of thousands of Bolton and West Ham fans gained illegal entry to the first Wembley final in 1923, in the days when the season's showpiece was not an all-ticket affair. When floodlighting was introduced, some supporters, such as these at Craven Cottage, inevitably saw them as ready-made gantries affording an uninterrupted view.

ROYAL PATRONAGE

Above: Tom Finney introduces the Preston team to the Queen Mother before the 1954 FA Cup final. Opponents West Bromwich Albion, who finished runners-up to Wolves that season, won 3-2.

Opposite: The Duke of York meets Huddersfield Town's players prior to the 1922 Cup Final, in which they played Preston at Stamford Bridge. His father, King George V, had become the first reigning monarch to watch the showpiece event when he attended the Burnley-Liverpool final at Crystal Palace in 1914. A disputed penalty won this game for Huddersfield, Bruce Grobbelaar-like antics from Preston 'keeper Mitchell failing to put off Town's England winger Billy Smith. The club's first silverware came two years after Herbert Chapman took over as manager; he went on to steer Huddersfield to two championships.

HUNGARIANS END ENGLAND RUN

Right: Billy Wright exchanges pennants with Ferenc Puskas prior to the England-Hungary match at Wembley on 25 November 1953. England had lost just once in the previous two years – against Uruguay in Montevideo – and had never been beaten at home by Continental opposition. Hungary's record was even more impressive: the Magyars were on an undefeated run stretching back to May 1950. A hat-trick from the outstanding deep-lying centre-forward Nandor Hidegkuti paved the way for Hungary's 6-3 victory, regarded by many as one of the finest footballing exhibitions of all time. The Hungarians would carry all before them for another two years, including a 7-1 demolition of England in a return match in Budapest. Their single defeat in 48 matches over a five-year period came in the 1954 World Cup final, in which Hungary went down 3-2 to West Germany.

Left: The Arsenal and Moscow Spartak captains check the outcome of a toss-up. Wolves' victory over Spartak in 1954 led to claims that the Midlands club were the uncrowned champions of Europe. This was the catalyst for the introduction of the European Cup, first played in 1955-56.

THE GALLOPING MAJOR

Opposite: Ferenc Puskas is an honoured guest at a reception in 1957, the year following the Hungarian Revolution. Puskas had been out of the country with Honved at the time of the uprising and, along with several of his team-mates, chose not to return. The 29-year-old Galloping Major was thought past his best and overlooked by a number of clubs before signing for Real Madrid. He scored four goals in the

famous 7-3 victory over Eintracht Frankfurt in the 1960 European Cup final, and played top-level football until he was 39.

Above: Johnny Haynes, Johnny Byrne and Alan Mullery at Lilleshall, preparing for the 1962 World Cup. Walter Winterbottom's men were unconvincing in reaching the last eight, where they went down 3-1 to eventual winners Brazil.

CHARLTON REACH WEMBLEY DESPITE LOSING TIE

Opposite: Charlton's Ben Fenton receiving treatment from club trainer Jimmy Trotter in 1949. Charlton made successive Cup Final appearances in 1946 and 1947. They won the latter, the club's only success in the competition, but it was the previous year which provided a quirk for the record books. With no league programme, it was decided to make Cup matches up to the semi-final stage two-legged affairs. In the third round Charlton lost 2-1 away to Fulham but won on aggregate, making them the only club to be defeated and still reach Wembley.

Above: Blackburn full-back Dave Whelan suffers a broken leg during the 1960 Cup Final, against Wolves. In the pre-substitute era the loss of the future sportwear entrepreneur was a major blow to Rovers, who went down 3-0.

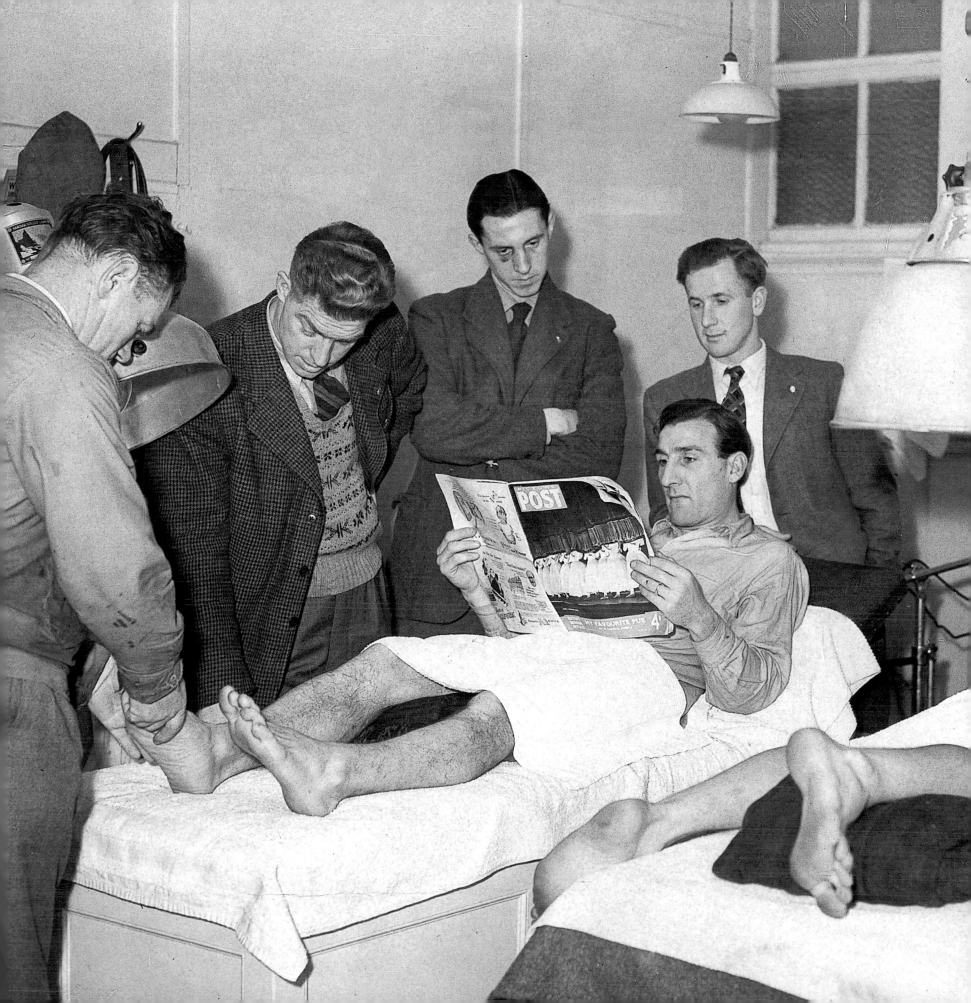

HISTORIC WIN FOR NORTHERN IRELAND

Opposite: 6 November 1957: Jubilant Northern Ireland players leave the pitch after an historic first victory over England at Wembley. Two months later a magnificent 2-1 win over Italy in Belfast clinched Northern Ireland's place at the 1958 World Cup. Managed by Peter Doherty and led on the field by the inspirational Danny Blanchflower, the team won a group play-off against Czechoslovakia to reach the quarter-final, further than either England or Scotland. France proved a hurdle too far for an exhausted and injury-hit squad, Northern Ireland going down valiantly 4-0. Just Fontaine added two more goals to a tally that would eventually reach 13, a World Cup record.

Above: A game at Bristol City is suspended when spectators spill over onto the pitch. In the 19th century football had been championed by the great public schools but it soon took over from the handling code as the sport of the masses. After the two world wars in particular, crowds flocked to football as a cheap form of escapism from post-conflict austerity.

BABES AT PLAY

Above: Manchester United players while away the journey to London for a league fixture in 1957. United won the championship by 11 points in 1955-56, retaining the title by an eight-point margin the following season, racking up 103 goals. Matt Busby bought just three players – Tommy Taylor, Johnny Berry and 'keeper Ray Wood – to add to his crop of home-grown stars (l-r: McGuinness, Foulkes, Jones, Colman, Wood).

Opposite: Aspiring men in black sign up for a course run by the London Society of Referees.

SUPERSTARS AND CELEBRITIES

Opposite: The incomparable George Best, arguably the most naturally gifted player the game has ever produced. Manchester United manager Matt Busby certainly thought so; he famously instructed the Old Trafford coaching staff not to try and teach the 15-year-old Belfast boy anything when he first saw the prodigious skills in action in the autumn of 1961. Best made his first-team debut when he was 17, and after just 15 appearances in a United shirt he was selected for Northern Ireland. Although destined never to grace a World Cup, Best produced some stellar performances on the European stage. One such came in a 5-1 away win against Benfica in the 1965-6 European Cup, after which he was dubbed 'El Beatle'. Best had a pop star image; with a champagne lifestyle and succession of beautiful girlfriends he made good copy beyond the sporting pages of the newspapers. By the age of 22 he had helped United to two league titles and victory in the European Cup. He won the 1968 European Footballer of the Year award, yet just four years later, at 26, his career began its long slide. Goldfish-bowl pressures and the belief that an ageing United side should have been broken up and rebuilt around him were contributory factors, as was the tendency for Best to press the self-destruct button all too often.

Right: Billy Meredith, whose dazzling wing play at the turn of the twentieth century earned him the nickname the 'Welsh Wizard'. Like Best, Meredith was regarded as the superstar of his day. He began his career with Manchester City in 1894 and didn't hang up his boots until defeat in the FA Cup semi-final of 1924, when he was just a few months short of his 50th birthday. In between his two stints with City, Meredith enjoyed a highly successful spell with rivals United. He won the FA Cup with both clubs, scoring the only goal of the game when City met Bolton in 1904, then helping United to victory over Bristol City in 1909. He also won two championships with United, in 1908 and 1911. The single blot on a remarkable career was an allegation that he attempted to bribe an Aston Villa player in a key match at the end of the 1904-5 season. It earned him an eight-month ban but not any silverware; City and Villa finished 3rd and 4th respectively in the title race.

ANY SPECTATORS GOT THEIR BOOTS WITH THEM?

Opposite: A section of the White Hart Lane faithful waiting for their team to take on Millwall in March 1940. Hostilities had brought the league programme proper to an end early in the 1939-40 season. However, as in the First World War, it was quickly recognised that football could play an important part in boosting morale in a time of crisis. Obviously, player availability was a major headache for the fixture organisers. It was not unknown for teams to bolster their depleted numbers from the ranks of the opposition – sometimes even the crowd!

Above: Wolves and Grimsby supporters on the the pitch in a 1939 match.

UP FOR THE CUP

Left: Die-hard Tottenham fan, 1920s style. Spurs began their great love affair with years ending in '1' by lifting the 1901 FA Cup, their first victory in the competition. In beating Sheffield United 3-1 after a replay, Spurs became the first non-league side to win the trophy, a feat that it is hard to imagine will ever be emulated. Although Spurs had recently won the Southern League championship, the club would have to wait seven more years before joining the elite. Spurs were elected to the league in 1908, gaining promotion to the top flight at the first attempt. The club's only silverware in the 1920s came exactly 20 years after the maiden success. The 1-0 win over Wolves in 1921 marked the end of an era of dominance by northern and Midlands clubs, who had won the Cup in each of the intervening years.

Opposite: An ardent Wolves fan goes in for a distinctive brand of neckwear by way of exhorting his team to give of their best. One of the 12 founder members of the Football League, Wolves won the Cup in 1893 and 1908. When they reached the final in 1939, Wolves were odds-on to make it a hat-trick. The team, marshalled by the great Stan Cullis at centre-half, were championship runners-up but crashed 4-1 to a Portsmouth side languishing in the bottom half of the table. Legend has it that the Wolves players were so nervous the autographs they signed that day were illegible. By contrast, the Portsmouth players were treated to pre-match entertainment from a comedian and went on to the pitch refreshed and relaxed.

NEVER, REF!

Opposite: Leeds United's fiery captain Billy Bremner was invariably in the thick of the action, whether confronting opposing players or putting his point across to referees. Here he takes Ken Burns to task over a disallowed goal against Chelsea in the FA Cup semi-final of 1966-67. Leeds lost the match 1-0. Bremner epitomised Leeds' rise to the top in the 1960s: a ferocious competitor who asked and gave no quarter; a player reviled by most rival fans but one whom they would undoubtedly have liked to see turn out for their own team. Under manager Don Revie, who arrived when the club was flirting with relegation to the Third Division, Leeds became one of the most feared and respected sides in Europe. The championship went to Elland Road in 1969 and 1974; in the former season the club set a new record of 67 points and just two defeats in the 42-match programme. Leeds also lifted the FA Cup, League Cup and twice won the Inter-Cities Fairs Cup. Yet they were far more often the nearly men: five times runners-up in the championship and with three FA Cup final defeats, Leeds also finished on the losing side in each of the three European competitions.

Right: Dissent 1930s style, which in this instance seems to be part pleading, part resignation. Indiscipline – and its consequences – was very different from the modern era. Games were more physical, sometimes bordering on violent, and considerable licence was given before the officials intervened. When England took on world champions Italy in November 1934, the game was punctuated by some savage tackling. England captain Eddie Hapgood was among the walking wounded at the end of the match: he suffered a broken nose, courtesy of an Italian elbow. It ended 3-2 to England, and with 22 players still on the pitch.

SILKY SPURS WIN QUAGMIRE BATTLE

Opposite: Even in the 1920s Spurs were associated with the artistry of the beautiful game. This spectacular effort by Bert Bliss in the 1921 FA Cup final against Wolves was off target, although quagmire conditions at Stamford Bridge weren't conducive to flowing football and silky skills.

Above: Bliss tries a more conventional effort on goal. The game was settled in Spurs' favour by a second-half strike from winger Jimmy Dimmock. Sixth place in the league and a second FA Cup victory represented a fine showing for a team that had just bounced back from a season in Division Two. This was also the year in which the Southern League en bloc became the Third Division, the league now consisting of 66 clubs.

ARTISAN AND ARTIST

Opposite: Frank Barson, a rugged, uncompromising defender, one of the most feared – and oft-suspended players of the interwar years. Barson played over 350 league matches in a 20-year career, a decade of which was spent at Aston Villa. Barson won the FA Cup with Villa in 1920, the year in which he was awarded his one and only England cap. This was the era in which the centre-half was the pivotal player with a more attacking role. Barson fulfilled it admirably, on one occasion scoring with a bullet header from 30 yards. Manchester United saw him as a key acquisition after the club finished bottom of Division One in 1921-22. Barson moved to Old Trafford for a fee of £5,000, and was promised a public house if United won promotion back to the top flight within three years. After finishing 4th and 14th, United were runners-up in 1924-25. Barson duly claimed his prize, although his tenure was short-lived; he instantly decided that the lot of a publican wasn't for him.

Left: Jimmy Greaves, arguably the most lethal finisher in British football in the 1960s. Gary Lineker's 48 international goals relegated Greaves to third in the all-time list of England goalscorers. But Lineker's haul came from 80 appearances, while top-ranked Bobby Charlton scored his 49 goals in 106 matches. Greaves' return of 44 goals came from just 57 appearances, a far superior strike rate than that of the two illustrious names above him in the list. Greaves' nine years at White Hart Lane saw him at his most prolific. He scored 220 league goals, including 37 in 1962-63, setting new Spurs records with both. His 1962-63 haul made him the First Division's hotshot, a title he retained for the following two seasons. He had also twice topped the scoring charts for Chelsea in the late 1950s.

THE PRESTON PLUMBER

Above: The great Tom Finney battling with atrocious conditions at Stamford Bridge in 1956. Finney, who spent his entire playing career at Preston, was a versatile and potent forward, capable of playing on either wing or through the middle. Another of Deepdale's famous sons, Bill Shankly, famously once said that Finney would have been outstanding in any era - even wearing an overcoat. The unassuming

Finney – known as the Preston Plumber – hit a record 187 league goals for the club, and netted 30 times for England in 76 matches. He won the Footballer of the Year award in 1954 and 1957.

Opposite: Chelsea and Bolton play a game more akin to water polo at Stamford Bridge in February 1957. Champions two years earlier, Chelsea spent six seasons mid-table before being relegated in 1961-62.

THE CAT

Above: A superbly acrobatic save from Sheffield Wednesday's Ron Springett keeps out Arsenal in a match at Highbury at the start of the 1959-60 season. Newly promoted Wednesday, who won 1-0, had the best defensive record in Division Two the previous season, and only three teams conceded fewer goals this term in the top flight, the Yorkshire club finishing fifth and reaching the semis of the FA Cup.

Springett won 33 caps between 1960 and 1966, a figure which would undoubtedly have been higher had he not been a contemporary of Gordon Banks.

Opposite: More goalkeeper acrobatics this time in the 1961 international game between England and Wales.

ROVERS EQUAL VILLA'S RECORD

Above: Blackburn Rovers players show off the FA Cup after their 3-1 win over Huddersfield in the 1928 final. The Lancashire club had finished either as league champions or runners-up five years running. Victory to mid-table Rovers, thanks to a brace from Roscamp and one from McLean, was thus against the form book. It was Blackburn's sixth FA Cup success – equalling Villa's record – and would be the club's last silverware until the championship-winning season 1994-95.

Opposite: Bill Shankly guards the FA Cup as he returns to Liverpool following his team's 3-0 victory over Newcastle United at Wembley in 1974. The final brought down the curtain on a glorious 15-year reign.

THE KHAKI CUP FINAL

Above and opposite: The 1914-15 league and cup programme was completed, but with little relish as hostilities had been under way for several months. Initially the authorities thought football was the ideal distraction from the horrors of war, but when it became clear that there would be no quick victory, it was decided to suspend the normal programme, although regional football continued throughout the conflict. Everton won the championship, though just six points covered the top 11 teams. Chelsea weren't among those – they finished second bottom, but beat the Merseysiders in the FA Cup semi-final. They went down 3-0 to Sheffield United in the final, held at Old Trafford. Many of the 50,000-strong crowd were servicemen, and the match would go down in the annals as the 'Khaki Final'.

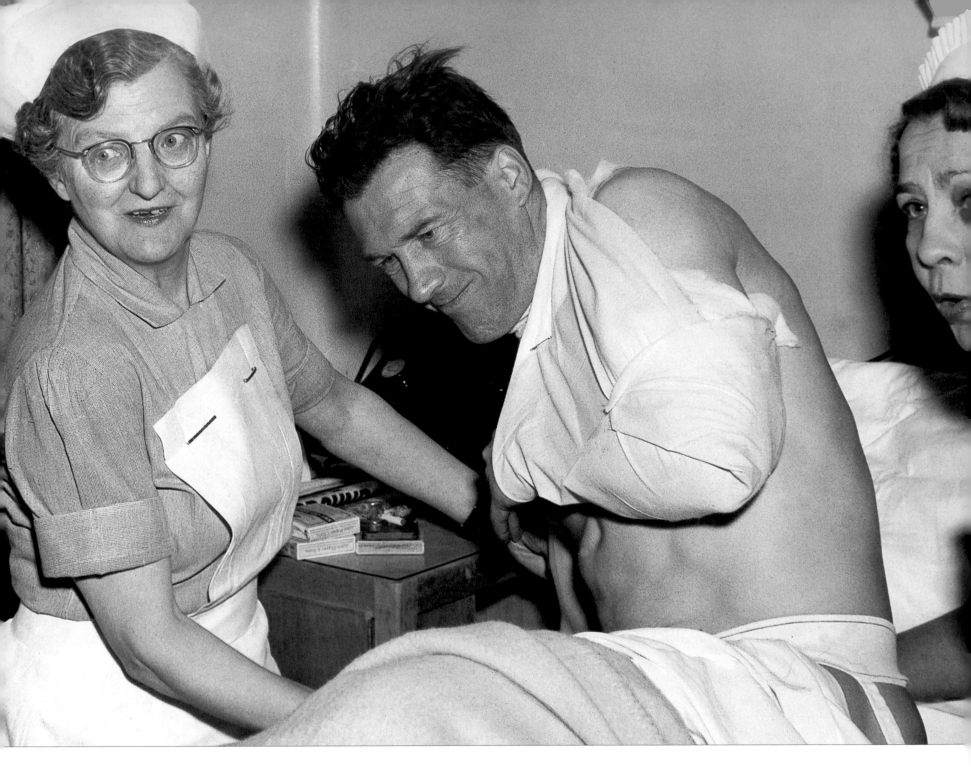

DRAKE JOINS EXCLUSIVE CLUB

Opposite: Arsenal centre-forward Ted Drake receiving infra-red treatment on a leg injury. The acquisition of Drake helped Arsenal maintain their supremacy after the death of manager Herbert Chapman in 1934. His prolific scoring record for Southampton prompted Chapman's successor George Allison to pay £6,500 for him that year. In his first full season Drake hit 42 goals in 41 games; it made him the division's top marksman and set a Highbury record which still stands. Drake notched six goals in

his five appearances for England but was in his mid-30s by the time football resumed after the Second World War. He turned to management, guiding Chelsea to the 1955 championship. He remains one of only nine men to have played in and managed a championship-winning team.

Above: Bolton legend Nat Lofthouse. His 30 international goals were equalled by Alan Shearer, but the latter took 30 more matches to reach that target.

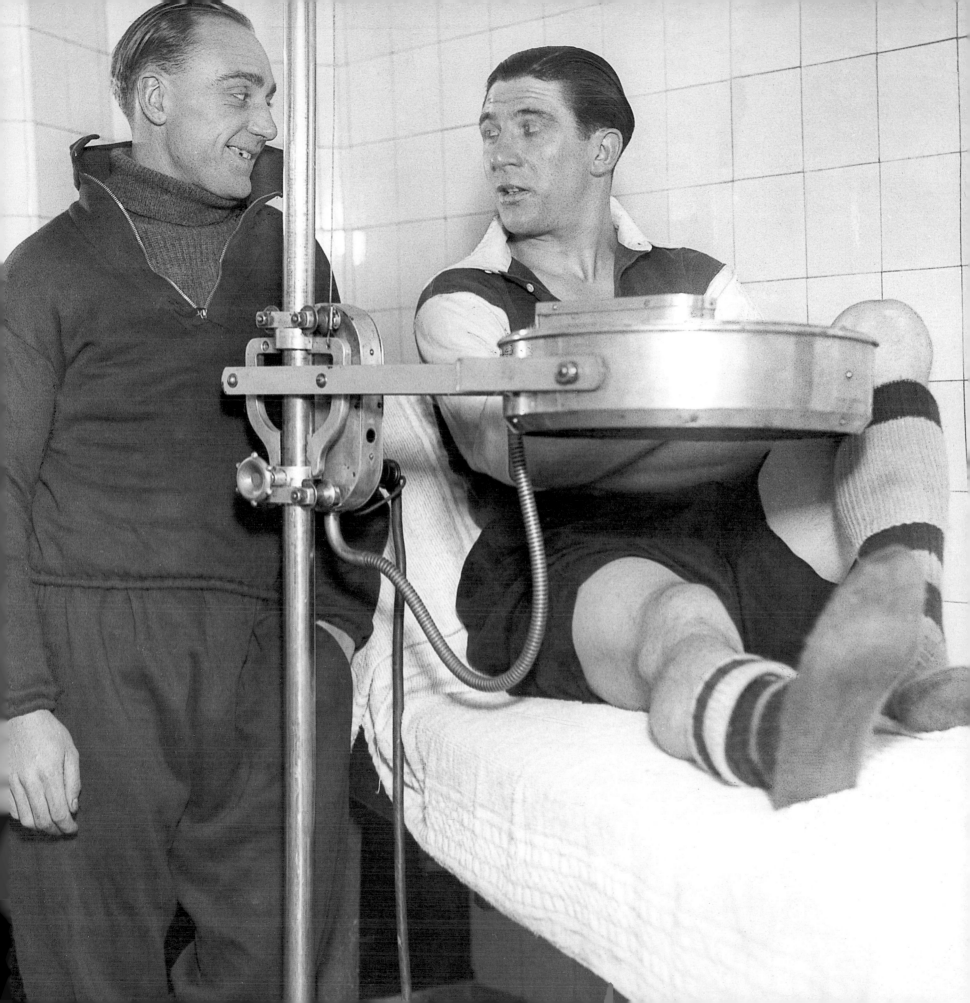

THE MATTHEWS FINAL

Above: The Queen presents Stan Matthews with his winners' medal following Blackpool's amazing 4-3 victory over Bolton in the 1953 FA Cup final. Matthews had finished on the losing side twice in the previous five years, and when Bolton took a 3-1 second-half lead it seemed as if the 38-year-old maestro was destined for further disappointment. He had a hand in all three goals which turned the match on its head, notably the injury-time cross which Perry

converted. The outpouring of joy for Matthews eclipsed the fact that Stan Mortensen had become the first man to score a hat-trick in a Wembley final.

Opposite: Aston Villa get their hands on the Cup for a sixth time in 1920. The goal which beat Huddersfield was scored by Bill Kirton, bought for a song from Leeds City, who had been expelled from the league for making illegal payments to players.

PRETENDERS TO THE CROWN

Left: Burnley 'keeper Adam Blacklaw at full stretch as he keeps out an effort from Spurs' Cliff Jones at White Hart Lane in October 1958. Both had finished in the top six in the previous campaign; both were about to win the championship. Burnley took the title in 1960, though reigning champions Wolves ran them very close. Both won 24 matches, but Burnley drew 7, one more than Cullis' men, to top the table by a point. Burnley hadn't led the division until the last day of the season. Spurs inherited the mantle the following year, winning far more comfortably. Bill Nicholson's team reeled off 11 straight wins at the start of the season, finishing the season with 31 victories, 16 of them away from home. No other club had so dominated a 42-match programme, introduced when the league was extended to 22 clubs in 1919-20.

Opposite: Shrewsbury win at Watford in May 1959 to clinch promotion to Division Three. The Shrews' player-manager Arthur Rowley hit 38 goals; he is league football's record marksman, with 434 goals to his name.

PLAYER POWER

Above: Fulham's Jimmy Hill finds himself in the back of the net with an Everton defender in a Division One match during the 1959-60 season. Hill, chairman of the Professional Footballers Association since 1957, was at the forefront of the campaign which resulted in the abolition of the £20-a-week maximum wage in 1961. The PFA also negotiated an end to the 'retain and transfer' system which bound players to clubs. In a celebrated case which foreshadowed the Bosman ruling some 30 years later, George Eastham took Newcastle United to court over the club's refusal to grant his transfer request. The decision went in Eastham's favour, the judge deciding that he had been the victim of an unreasonable restraint of trade.

Opposite: Jubilation at Portman Road as Alf Ramsey's Ipswich Town edge one step closer to winning the championship in 1961-62, the club's first season in Division One.

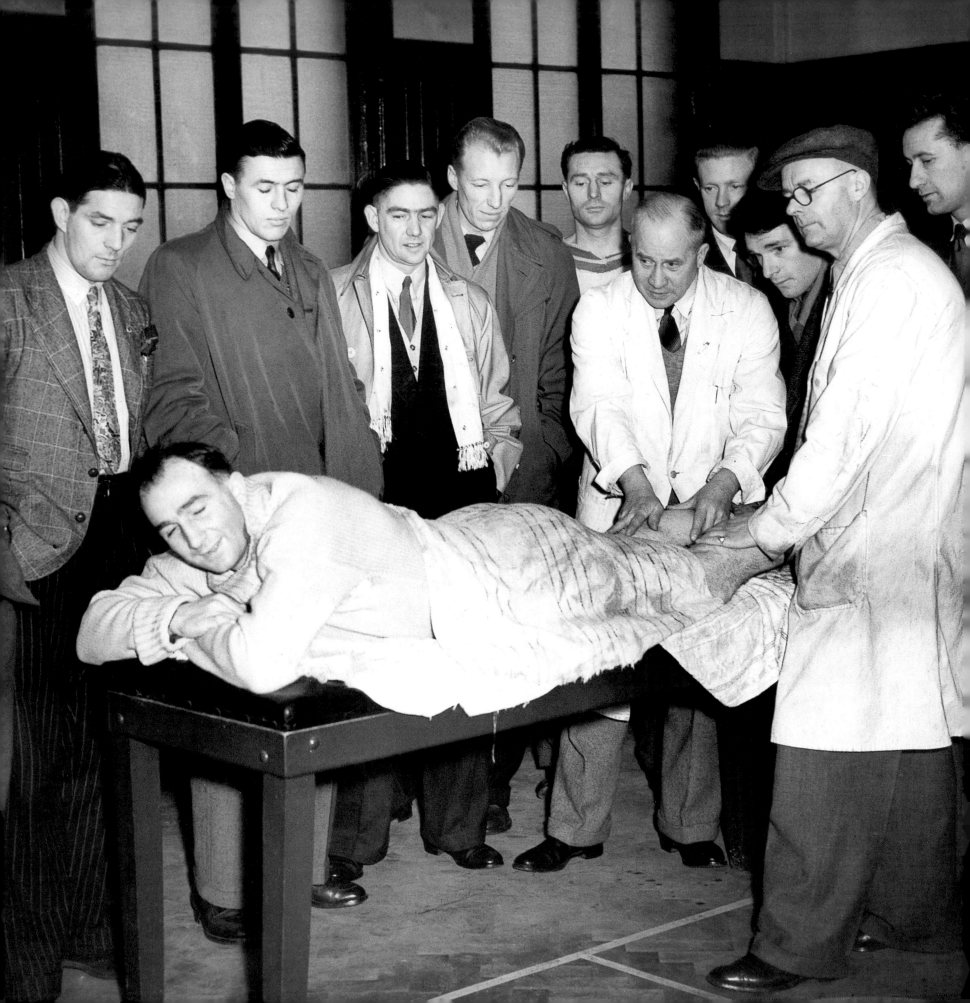

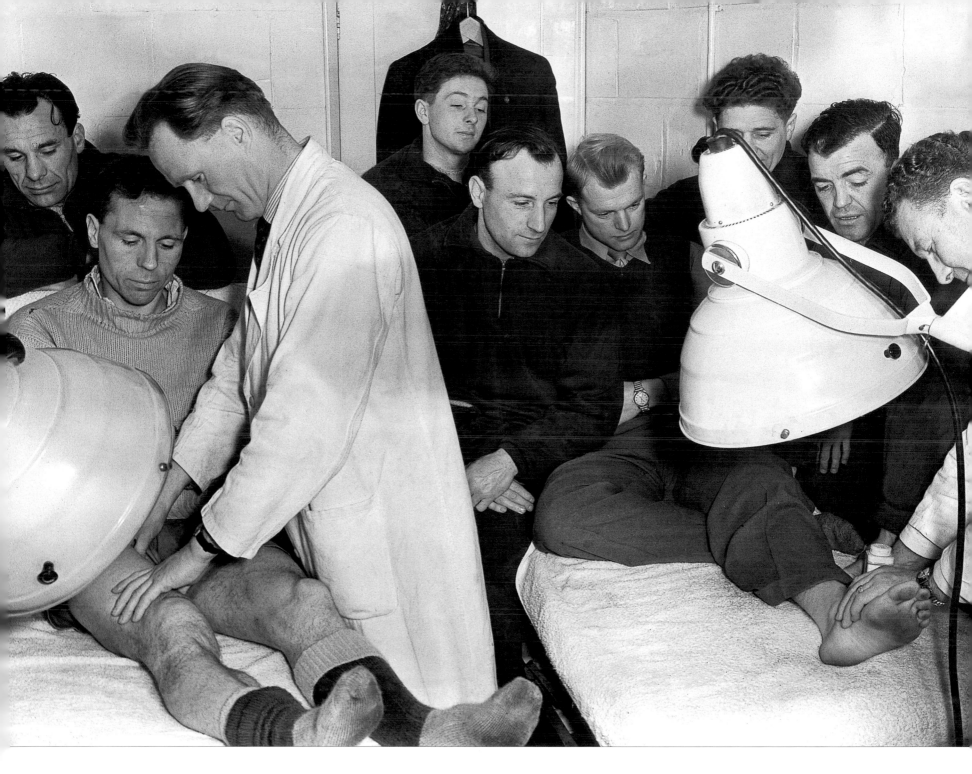

TEAM OF THE 50s

Opposite: Aston Villa's Harry Parkes gets a rub-down, with some of his team-mates looking on. They were preparing for a fourth-round FA Cup derby against Wolves in the 1950-51 season. Wolves won the match 3-1. While Villa lifted the trophy for a record seventh time in 1957, they were a long way from emulating the heady achievements of the turn of the century. Wolves, by contrast, vied with Manchester United as the team of the decade. The Midlands club finished in the top three on seven occasions in the 1950s, winning the championship three times. Busby's team played the kind of football which the purist could admire; Stan Cullis believed in getting the ball into the box quickly and often, and he achieved remarkable success with this style of play.

Above: It's standing room only in the Birmingham City treatment room in March 1953.

CELEBRATING DEFEAT – AND THE CHAMPIONSHIP

Above: Champagne celebrations don't usually follow defeat, but in this case it was well merited. Non-league Bedford Town made mighty Arsenal work hard for their place in the 1955-56 fourth-round FA Cup draw. Bedford took the Gunners to a replay, in which they went down only 2-1. They did better than six-times Cup winners Aston Villa, who were thumped 4-1 by Arsenal in the next round. The other big giant-killing story of the season was Boston's 6-1 rout of Derby County on the league side's own turf. The Rams had had a lean time of things since winning the first post-war Cup final, having been relegated twice in three seasons to find themselves in the Third Division (North), but it was still a shock result.

Opposite: Roger Byrne pours the bubbly as Manchester United toast their second postwar championship. United finished 11 points clear of the pack, equalling Aston Villa's feat of 1896-97.

'KEEPER INJURIES PROMPT CLAMOUR FOR SUBSTITUTES

Opposite: Injury to Birmingham City's international 'keeper just three minutes into a league match against Chelsea early in the 1957-58 season once again prompted many commentators to call for the introduction of substitutes. The Stamford Bridge incident came just weeks after a Peter McParland challenge on Manchester United's Ray Wood in the Cup Final almost certainly robbed Busby's team of completing the double in 1956-57.

Above: Spurs' goalkeeper Ditchburn and Groves of Arsenal receive treatment after clashing in a derby fixture in October 1957. Spurs were entering a period of ascendancy over their north London rivals. In the 12 seasons beginning in 1956-57 the Gunners finished higher in the league only once, and were often to be found in mid-table. Spurs were regular title challengers, although they won the championship just once, the glorious double-winning campaign of 1960-61.

GOAL-FEST FOR VILLA FANS

Above: A sea of fans pictured at a league clash between arch-rivals Aston Villa and Birmingham City at Villa Park in October 1930. Although the Blues got a point that day, they were battling relegation, while Villa finished runners-up to mighty Arsenal. The Gunners set a new record that season by notching 66 points. They lost just four games, one of those a 5-1 mauling at Villa. The Midlands club did outdo Arsenal by hitting 128 goals, a new league record. Pongo Waring found the net on 49 occasions, making him the division's hotshot.

Arsenal, by contrast, shared out their goal tally between them. Cliff Bastin (28), David Jack (31) and Jack Lambert (38) were the major contributors. Arsenal ended the campaign having scored one goal fewer than Villa but with seven points more.

Opposite: Bolton and Portsmouth fans at the 1929 Cup Final. Bolton won the Cup for the third time in seven years, despite losing their star player. England inside-forward David Jack joined Arsenal for £10,890, doubling the previous transfer record.

THE INTER-CITIES FAIRS CUP

Left: West Bromwich Albion forward John Kaye gets in some target practice before the second leg of the club's third-round tie against Bologna in the Inter-Cities Fairs Cup. It proved a hurdle too far for Albion, who were 3-0 down from the first game in Italy. Bologna themselves went out in the next round, to Leeds United on the toss of a coin. Leeds lost to Dinamo Zagreb in the final, but a Mick Jones goal gave Don Revie's team victory over Ferencvaros the following year, the Yorkshire club's first success on the European stage. The Fairs Cup had begun life in 1955. It was conceived as a competition to coincide with the hosting of trade or industrial fairs. Cities were able to field representative sides, selecting players from a number of clubs. The first competition took three years to complete and the link with trade fairs was soon broken. It was relaunched as the UEFA Cup in 1971-72.

Opposite: Coventry players being put through their paces in 1955. At one time coaches deliberately starved players of the ball during training, hoping they would be fresh and hungry on match days.

VANTAGE POINT

Above: These spectators got a free view of the 1914 Cup Final from vantage points outside Crystal Palace. The last of the 20 finals to be played at this venue saw Burnley beat Liverpool 1-0. At the start of the season several rule changes were made: goalkeepers were required to play in distinctive colours; they could now use their hands only within the penalty area; and at free kicks opponents had to retire 10 yards.

Opposite: Floodlights and scoreboards provide the perfect view for these fans in 1957.

FOOTBALL STOPS FOR NOTHING

Above: Wolves 'keeper Bert Williams saves from Eddie Firmani but Charlton centre-forward Hewie follows up to score. It was but a consolation as reigning champions Wolves ran out 4-1 winners. They lost to Sunderland in the next round, while Chelsea edged Stan Cullis' team into second place in the league.

Opposite: A submerged White Hart Lane, January 1954. Incredibly, the game took place, Spurs beating Second Division side Leeds 1-0 in a third-round FA Cup tie. They went down 3-0 to eventual winners West Brom in the sixth round.

GREENWOOD DOES IT HIS WAY

Opposite: West Ham preparing for their sixth-round FA Cup tie with Burnley, February 1964. Manager Ron Greenwood had been under fire for taking his team on ambitious close-season tours, which had been followed by faltering starts in the league. Greenwood insisted the experience would bear fruit, putting Geoff Hurst's goal return down to the experience of playing against tight Continental defences. The Hammers beat Burnley 3-2 and went on to win the Cup for the first time.

Above: Arsenal in training for the 1962-63 season.

ROOT AND BRANCH CHANGE TO ENGLAND SET-UP

Opposite: Walter Winterbottom briefs his England players prior to the match against Northern Ireland at Wembley in November 1959, which they won 2-1. Winterbottom, a former Manchester United centre-half, had been appointed in 1946. Although he was charged with preparing the national team, selection remained in the hands of an unwieldy committee. Training was undemanding, organisation haphazard. Matthews missed the start of the 1950 World Cup as he was on an FA tour of Canada, and there was no team doctor to treat a sick Peter Swan at the 1962 World Cup.

Above. Alf Ramsey took the helm following a disappointing showing in Chile. The man who had guided Ipswich to the championship insisted on power as well responsibility. His professional approach paved the way for the 1966 triumph.

YOUNG FANS

Above: A young Manchester United fan meets star player Bobby Charlton and manager Matt Busby. The Munich air crash left Busby with Harry Gregg, Bill Foulkes and the young Charlton around which to rebuild. Charlton's record 106 England caps was eventually overhauled by Moore and Shilton, his record of 49 international goals has yet to be bettered.

Opposite: Nat Lofthouse with his children in 1959. An old-fashioned centre-forward, Lofthouse spent his entire career at Bolton Wanderers.

SKY BLUES END SPURS' RECORD

Left: Millwall's Jimmy Whitehouse falls victim to a pincer movement from Coventry's John Smith and Brian Hill in a Third Division match during the 1963-64 season. Coventry, who had had a season in the newly created Division Four in 1958-59, ended the year as champions. Three years later, 1966-67, the Midlands club won promotion to the top flight for the first time in its history. Although Coventry regularly flirted with relegation in the following decades, the club survived in the First Division – and the Premiership – for 34 years until relegation finally came in the 2000-01 season. That period did bring the club an FA Cup win over Spurs in 1987. The Sky Blues twice came from behind, and a shot deflected off Gary Mabbutt gave them a famous 3-2 victory, Spurs' first defeat in eight Wembley appearances. It remains the only major honour for a club which began life in 1895 as a works team for Singer bicycles before being elected to the league in 1919.

Opposite: Burnley and Fulham battling for a place in the 1962 FA Cup final. Burnley won 2-1 after a replay but went down to Spurs at Wembley.

AERIAL POWER

Opposite: The Swansea defence finds that even at 32 Tommy Lawton still represents a spring-heeled danger. Lawton, who bagged a hat-trick on his debut for Burnley in 1936, aged 17, went on to star for Everton, Chelsea and Notts County. He also scored 22 goals in 23 England appearances. In 1952 he joined Division Two side Brentford as player-manager, before returning to the top flight for a fine twilight spell with Arsenal.

Above: Manchester United's Tommy Taylor, bought from Barnsley by Matt Busby for £1 short of £30,000.

BACK-TO-BACK TITLES FOR PUSH-AND-RUN SPURS

Above: North London derby early in the 1950-51 season. Spurs, having just been promoted as Division Two winners, made it successive championships with their great push-and-run side.

Opposite: Newcastle 'keeper Simpson gets to the ball ahead of Villa inside-forward Dixon in a 1956-57 league clash. United were inconsistent in the league in the 1950s but were the form team in the Cup, winning it three times in five years. The club's 1955 win over Manchester City was their sixth and most recent success in the competition.

THIRD TIME LUCKY FOR SAUNDERS

Opposite: Aston Villa manager Ron Saunders inspects the Wembley pitch prior to the 1975 League Cup final against Norwich. Saunders had been in charge of the Norwich side which had lost to Spurs two years earlier, and suffered a second disappointment as Manchester City boss in 1974. It was third time lucky in 1975, Ray Graydon hitting the only goal of the game.

Above: August 1958. Six months after the Munich air disaster Manchester United return to Germany to take part in a special thanksgiving match. United lost eight players in the crash. When they took on Sheffield Wednesday in the fifth round of the FA Cup two weeks later, the programme's team sheet had to be left blank. A makeshift side won the match and United went on to reach the final, but Bolton prevented a fairytale end to a tragic season.

HIGH TECHNOLOGY – AND ELBOW GREASE

Opposite: Engineers laying the cables for undersoil heating at Goodison Park in 1957. It wasn't until March of that year that Manchester United's floodlighting system was installed. Arsenal had blazed the trail for night-time football, hosting a friendly under lights during the 1951-52 season. The FA was initially sceptical, fearing that clubs would overreach themselves unnecessarily. The fans had no qualms; they took to floodlit football, although it was not until November 1963 that Wembley staged an entire international match under lights. England enjoyed the experience, beating Northern Ireland 8-3.

Above: The Arsenal boot room in the 1950s shows that technology hasn't pervaded all areas of football's infrastructure.

TRAUTMANN PLAYS THROUGH PAIN BARRIER

Opposite: Manchester City skipper Roy Paul leaves the royal box clutching the Cup after his team's 3-1 win over Birmingham City in the 1956 final. The game will forever be remembered for the heroics of City 'keeper Bert Trautmann, who had already picked up the Footballer of the Year award for performances which had helped City to fourth place in the league. He eclipsed that at Wembley by playing the last 15 minutes with a broken neck, sustained when he dived at the feet of Blues' Peter Murphy.

Left: The King signs autographs for two star-struck young United fans. A consummate goalscorer and showman, Law scored 236 goals in 399 appearances for United, helping the club to win the FA Cup and two league titles. Unlike Best and Charlton, he missed out on the Footballer of the Year award but was named Europe's top player in 1964. Law jointly holds the international scoring record for Scotland with Kenny Dalglish, though his 30 goals came from 55 games, Dalglish's from 102.

WAXING LYRICAL

Above: Burnley's John Connelly turns away after scoring for England against Sweden at Wembley, 28 October 1959. Bobby Charlton also got on the scoresheet but England went down 3-2. Bolton 'keeper Eddie Hopkinson had a nightmare, said to be the first England player to be jeered by home fans at Wembley. His international career came to an abrupt end shortly thereafter.

Opposite: Joy for Southend as Liverpool's Molineux puts through his own goal during a bruising third-round FA Cup tie in 1958. Liverpool won the tie 3-2, eventually falling to Blackburn in the sixth round. It was a lean time for Liverpool, who had been relegated in 1953-54, ending a 50-year run in the top flight.

THE WHITE HORSE FINAL

Opposite and above: A spectacular aerial view of the mayhem at the first Wembley FA Cup final. The stadium was built to house the 1924 British Empire Exhibition, but in order to guarantee regular use a 21-year deal was struck by which the Cup Final would be staged there. It was erected in just 300 days, at a cost of £750,000, and was ready for the 1923 final. Infantrymen tested the terracing, but the FA underestimated the number who would turn up to watch Bolton take on West Ham, then riding high in Division Two. The 126,000 capacity was soon reached and still the fans poured in, many by illicit means. PC George Scorey and his white horse Billy helped restore order. The game, which kicked off 40 minutes late, was won 2-0 by Bolton.

HAPPY HAMMERS

Above: 41 years after appearing in the first Wembley final, the Hammers finally get their hands on the FA Cup. As in 1923 the 1964 final pitted a mid-table Division One side against a team challenging for Second Division honours. This time it was West Ham who were the top-flight team, and Ron Greenwood's men beat Preston 3-2. It was no stroll, the Hammers twice coming from behind before Ron Boyce sealed victory with an injury-time winner. Preston's Howard Kendall picked up a losers' medal, and at 17 years 345 days became the youngest ever FA Cup finalist.

Opposite: West Ham's World Cup-winning trio (l-r) Geoff Hurst, Bobby Moore and Martin Peters.

LIVERPOOL TEAMS ON THE MARCH

Opposite: Having won their first FA Cup in 1906, Everton made it to Crystal Palace again the following year. In 1906 the Liverpudlians had upset the odds to defeat the team of the decade, Newcastle United, the three-times champions who also reached five FA Cup finals in seven years. In 1907 Everton were the favourites to beat mid-table Wednesday, but lost the match 2-1.

Above: Liverpool's first FA Cup final came with the storm clouds of war gathering over Europe. They met three Southern League sides before coming up against holders Villa in the semis of the 1913-14 competition. Victory set up a Crystal Palace encounter with Burnley, which the latter side won through a goal from Freeman.

FIRST ENGLAND-ARGENTINA BATTLE

Opposite: Argentina take the lead against England in the first fixture between the two countries, a Wembley clash on 9 May 1951. Goals from Mortensen and Milburn in the last quarter of an hour turned the game round for England.

Left: Two weeks earlier the England strike duo had been on opposite sides in the Cup Final. Milburn's Newcastle had come out on top against Mortensen's Blackpool that day, 'Wor Jackie' hitting both goals in a 2-0 victory and completing the set of a scoring in every round. The outcome might have been different had this terrific header from Stanley Matthews not been cleared off the line by Newcastle defender Cowell when the score was goalless.

THE FIRST £100-A-WEEK PLAYER

Opposite: A Johnny Haynes body-swerve takes him away from three Liverpool defenders in a Division Two match early in the 1957-58 season. Fulham and Liverpool both challenged for promotion that year but came up just short. Bill Shankly's arrival and the beginning of the great Anfield resurgence was still two years away. While Shankly turned Liverpool into one of the most formidable sides in the land, perennially chasing major honours, Haynes remained at Craven Cottage and ended his 18-year career at the club empty-handed.

Left: 15-year-old Haynes shows his skills to his England Schoolboy team-mates in 1950. Haynes scored on his debut for the senior team against Northern Ireland in 1954. His international days were ended prematurely after a serious road accident in 1962, but he spent eight more years at the Cottage before winding down his career in South Africa. His loyalty to Fulham was rewarded in 1961, when he became the first £100-a-week footballer following the abolition of the maximum wage.

WARTIME INTERNATIONALS

Above: England meet Scotland at Wembley on 4 October 1941. The two countries contested 15 wartime internationals, England winning 11, with two draws and two defeats. The vagaries of the selection system – committee members lobbying for their personal favourites – meant that England fielded a huge number of players, many of them one-cap wonders. With fewer players available during the war, there was, ironically, greater consistency and continuity in selection matters.

Opposite: Burnley players dispute a Sheffield Wednesday goal awarded during the 1935 FA Cup semi-final. Wednesday won 3-0 and went on to beat WBA in the final.

SPURS WIN INAUGURAL UEFA CUP

Opposite: Spurs' stars Mike England, Alan Gilzean, Ralph Coates and
Joe Kinnear, with Martin Chivers behind, pose with the UEFA Cup. Two
goals from Chivers at Molineux helped Tottenham beat Wolves 3-2 on
aggregate in the inaugural competition, the UEFA Cup having replaced
the Fairs Cup that season.

Above: Sheffield Wednesday fans try to lay a hand on the hallowed FA
Cup following the team's dramatic 4-2 victory over WBA in the 1935 final.
With the game locked at 2-2 and looking to be heading for extra-time,
Wednesday winger Ellis Rimmer scored twice in the last three minutes. It
was the club's third, and most recent, success in the competition.

HAMMERS LEGEND

Above: Injured West Ham skipper Bobby Moore watches his team-mates being put through their paces during the 1968-69 season. Moore set a record by lifting trophies at Wembley in three successive years: the FA Cup in 1964, the Cup-Winners' Cup the following season and, of course, the World Cup in '66. His final Wembley appearance –

for Fulham against his old club in the 1975 final – ended in defeat. *Opposite:* Goodison Park, November 1961. The 1950s had been an indifferent decade for Everton, but under Harry Catterick the club consistently challenged for honours. Everton were champions in 1963 and 1970, and Cup winners in 1966.

POMPEY HOLD CUP FOR SEVEN YEARS

Opposite: Portsmouth captain Jimmy Guthrie is chaired off the field after Pompey's 4-1 win over Wolves in the 1939 Cup Final. Wolves had been 1-5 red-hot favourites; while they were finishing runners-up to Everton in the league, their opponents were just surviving a relegation battle. Wolves had scored 16 goals in the four games leading up to Wembley; Pompey's sole secret weapon seemed to be the lucky white spats worn by manager Jack Tinn throughout the cup run. The outbreak of war meant that Portsmouth would hold the trophy for seven years.

Right: Guthrie gets an escort and a rapturous homecoming as the Cup arrives on the south coast. It remains Pompey's only success in the competition, although the club did win back-to-back championships in 1949 and 1950.

FALTERING START FOR NEW CUP COMPETITION

Opposite: Aston Villa become first winners of the League Cup with a 3-2 aggregate victory over Rotherham. The competition got off to a stuttering start as Spurs, Sheffield Wednesday and Wolves – the top three sides in the league that year – were among those who declined to enter. The final moved to Wembley in 1967, when QPR beat West Brom 3-2, but it wasn't until 1969-70 that all 92 clubs entered the competition.

Above: A kiss for the FA Cup from Bobby Stokes, whose goal had given the Second Division club a shock 1-0 win over Manchester United in the 1976 final. Peter Osgood, a winner with Chelsea in 1970, looks on.

THE SHANKLY ERA

Opposite: Bill Shankly was revered by the Anfield faithful but never lost the common touch. Here he acknowledges the fans at the end of Liverpool's title-winning campaign of 1972-73, the third during his time at the helm. The Reds also beat Borussia Moenchengladbach in the UEFA Cup final, becoming the first club to win the championship and a European trophy in the same season. Shankly wanted to build a side so formidable that 'they'd have to send a team from bloody Mars to beat us'. The aim was near enough fulfilled under his successors.

Above: An adoring fan adorns Shankly with a Liverpool scarf as the great man bids farewell after 15 years at Anfield.

THE UNDERDOG BITES

Left: Sunderland boss Bob Stokoe embraces his match-winner Ian Porterfield after the team's sensational FA Cup victory over Leeds in 1973. In nine years Leeds had finished no lower than fourth in the league and had reached four cup finals. In the same period Sunderland had been a struggling Division One side, finally relegated in 1970. In upsetting the odds Sunderland became only the fifth Second Division club to lift the Cup. Southampton (1976) and West Ham (1980) have since added to that tally.

Opposite: 1978 Cup Final: Ipswich defenders Kevin Beattie and Mick Mills celebrate keeping a clean sheet against an Arsenal side that had finished 13 places above them in the league. Roger Osborne, the unlikely goal hero, was so overcome by the occasion that he had to be substituted by boss Bobby Robson. The Robson era also delivered a UEFA Cup victory in 1981, but runners-up to Villa that year and Liverpool the next was the club's best championship return. The Ramsey-led success of 1962 thus remains Ipswich's sole Division One title.

'FINEST ENGLISH PLAYER SINCE FINNEY'

Opposite: Kevin Keegan tussles for the ball with Birmingham's Kenny Burns at St Andrews in 1973. Keegan arrived at Anfield in the summer of 1971, a £35,000 buy from Fourth Division Scunthorpe. He scored seven minutes into his debut, the first of 68 goals in a six-year spell in which he lit up English football. Keegan won the 1976 Footballer of the Year award, and following his £500,000 move to Hamburg, was named as Europe's top player in 1978 and 1979. Shankly rated his bargain buy the greatest English player since Tom Finney.

Above: Archie Gemmill, a key member of Derby's championship winning side of 1971-72, harried by Spurs' Phil Beal.

THE SHANKLY LEGACY

Above: The 1971 Liverpool squad pictured with the architect of the club's success. In 12 years Bill Shankly had turned Liverpool from an average Second Division side into one of the most feared teams in Europe. He delivered three championships, two FA Cup victories and the club's first European trophy. However, this merely laid the foundation for even greater success after he stepped down following the demolition of Newcastle in the 1974 Cup Final.

Opposite: The FA Cup sits at the feet of Joe Mercer, who captained Arsenal to victory over Liverpool in the 1950 final. Mercer also won the Footballer of the Year award.

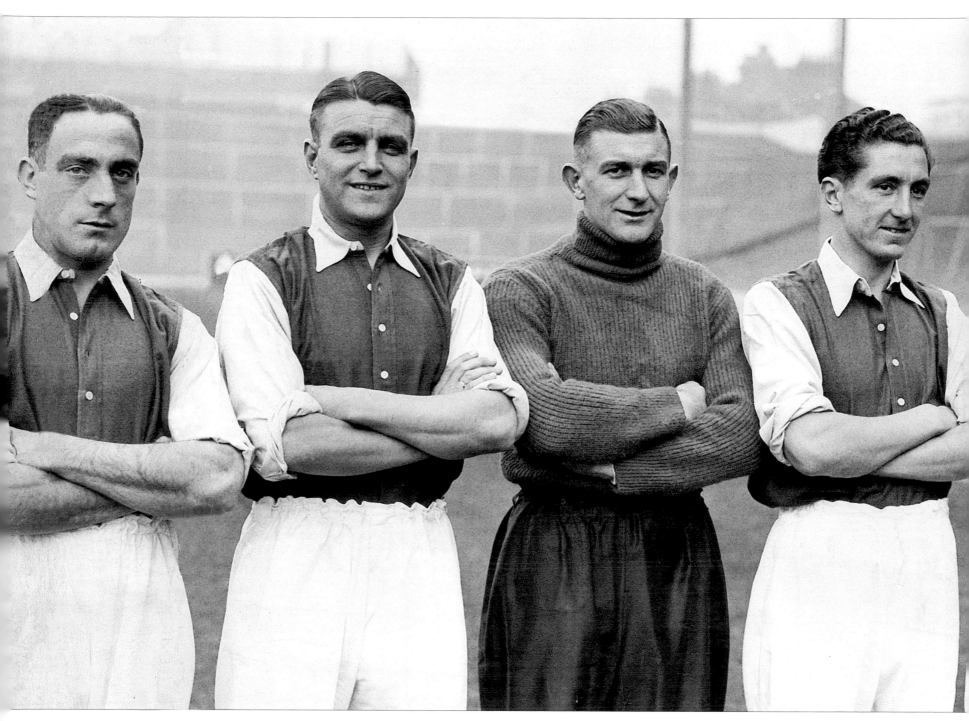

ENGLAND WIN 'BATTLE OF HIGHBURY'

Above: Arsenal's Copping, Hapgood, Moss and Bowden, four of the seven-strong Highbury contingent in the England side which took on world champions Italy on 14 November 1934. England won a brutal encounter 3-2, Ted Drake hitting what proved to be the decisive goal. Victory in the match dubbed the 'Battle of Highbury' meant that England's unbeaten home record against overseas opposition remained intact.

Opposite: Spurs' 1981-82 side included Argentine internationals Ricardo Villa and Ossie Ardiles (right and third from right), bought by Keith Burkinshaw after the 1978 World Cup. The Falklands War caused them to miss out on a second FA Cup victory, Spurs beating QPR 1-0 after a replay.

THE 'BOOT ROOM'

Left: Bill Shankly helps to pack the Carlisle kit before the team's departure for a cup game. Shankly cut his managerial teeth at Brunton Park, joining the Third Division (North) club in 1949. He had spells at Grimsby, Workington and Huddersfield before being targeted by Liverpool as the man to launch the Liverpool revival. At Anfield the famous 'boot room' became the stuff of legend: it was from here that the backroom team of Bob Paisley, Ronnie Moran, Joe Fagan and Reuben Bennett helped Shankly orchestrate Liverpool's phenomenal success.

Opposite: Bristol City players wait to be handed their kit prior to a 1955 fixture. After 16 seasons in the Third Division (South), City were promoted in 1954-55. A return to the Second Division was a far cry from the heady days of the Edwardian era. City were championship runners-up in 1907, just six years after admission to the league, and FA Cup finalists two years later. The club's most recent top-flight experience came in the late 1970s, but relegation three seasons running meant that by 1983 Ashton Gate was hosting Fourth Division football.

TOP TWO LEAGUE SIDES MEET IN CUP FINAL

Opposite: Aston Villa beat Sunderland 1-0 in the 1913 FA Cup final. The positions were reversed in the league, and this remained the only time the champions and runners-up contested the Cup Final until 1986, when Everton finished runners-up to Liverpool in both competitions.

Above: Manchester City take on Portsmouth at Maine Road in January 1936. It was a period of wildly fluctuating fortunes for the Mancunian

club: mid-table that year, their first league title the next, then relegation in 1937-38. City suffered the drop in an extraordinarily tight division in which just 16 points separated top from bottom. City came into existence in 1884 as Gorton AFC and had a seven-year spell as Ardwick FC before the name Manchester City was adopted in 1894.

THE TEAM OF THE 1920s

Opposite: Huddersfield's Smith beats the Preston 'keeper from the spot, the only goal of the 1922 Cup Final. Although the infringement was committed outside the box, few neutrals begrudged Huddersfield their victory. The Yorkshire club was the team of the 1920s, notching a hat-trick of league titles between 1924 and 1926. They also hold the dubious distinction of being the first league champions to drop into the bottom division. That came in 1974-75, when Huddersfield finished bottom of the Third Division.

Right: Spurs' centre-forward Cantrell rises between two Wolves defenders during the 1921 Cup Final, played on a Stamford Bridge mudbath. Spurs won 1-0. Only Manchester United and Arsenal have a better Cup pedigree than Spurs, though the Lilywhites have won eight of the nine finals they've reached. Only Wanderers can match that record, with five wins out of five during the 1880s.

SOUTHERN LEAGUE SIDE TOPPLES ROKERMEN

Above: Delirious Yeovil Town fans after their team take the lead against Sunderland in the fourth round of the 1948-49 FA Cup. Yeovil, who had already taken the scalp of Second Division Bury, beat the top-flight side 2-1. Manchester United brought them down to earth with a bump in round five with an 8-0 mauling.

Opposite: Overnight queuing for a north London derby in 1949. One Gunners fan records his team's two FA Cup victories, and the question mark would soon be replaced with a third success. Arsenal were drawn at home in every round in 1949-50 – even the two games they needed to beat Chelsea in the semis were played at White Hart Lane. A 2-0 win over Liverpool at Wembley meant they became the first club to lift the trophy without leaving the capital.

SPURS STARS BREAK RECORD

Right: Tottenham's Terry Dyson has a painful encounter with a concrete wall during a 1964 league derby against West Ham at Upton Park. Dyson, Spurs' hero in their 5-1 demolition of Atletico Madrid in the 1963 Cup-Winners' Cup final, played on but a weakened Spurs side finished on the wrong end of a 4-0 drubbing. A few months earlier, 12 October 1963, Tottenham set a record when seven of their players took the field in the home internationals: Greaves, Norman and Smith played in the England side against Wales, whose line-up included Cliff Jones; Brown, Mackay and White played for Scotland against Northern Ireland on the same day.

Opposite: Wolves 'keeper Bert Williams is injured in saving a penalty from Aston Villa's Republic of Ireland international Con Martin during a fourth-round FA Cup tie in 1951. Wolves won 3-1, and went on to reach the semis, where they lost to eventual winners Newcastle United. Williams had a distinguished international career, and was capped 24 times between 1949 and 1956. One of those caps came in Belo Horizonte at the 1950 World Cup, when England lost to the USA in one of the shock results of all time.

MAGNIFICENT MAGYARS

Opposite: Something had to give when England met Hungary at Wembley in 1953. Puskas and Co. were on a 25-match unbeaten run, while England had never lost at home against Continental opposition. Hungary's players were co-opted either into the army side Honved or Red Banner. They played a fluid style, the precursor of 'total football', which dazzled England that November day. Final score: England 3, Hungary 6.

Above: West Ham 'keeper Ernie Gregory lies face down in the Upton Park mud after deflecting a shot into his own net during a third-round cup tie against WBA in 1953. It opened the floodgates for one of the First Division's top sides, who ran out 4-1 winners. West Brom went just one round further, losing a titanic struggle against Chelsea that went to three replays.

WALES' GREATEST MOMENT

Opposite: A Welsh mascot sports the line-up which beat England 2-1 at Cardiff on 22 October 1955. The Wales side, boasting two world-class players in Ivor Allchurch and John Charles, enjoyed its greatest moment three years later, with a quarter-final appearance at the World Cup. It was a far cry from the 1890s, when the Corinthians were dispatched en masse to take on Wales while England played Northern Ireland on the same day. As recently as the 1930s it had been common for England players to be capped against the 'minor' home nations as compensation for missing out on major honours.

Above: No replica shirts on view but with their rosettes and rattles these Chelsea fans make sure their team gets colourful and noisy support.

ENGLAND BACK HOME SOONER THAN EXPECTED

Opposite: England's 1970 World Cup squad. With their new Ford cars and 'Back Home' at No. 1, Alf Ramsey's men went into the tournament in confident mood. Eight of the '66 Wembley heroes were still there, and many believed the squad overall was stronger. Many predicted an England-Brazil final, after a tight group encounter between the two sides, but in the last eight England threw away a two-goal lead against

West Germany. Peter Bonetti, in for Banks, had won all six of his previous six outings for England. He shouldered some of the blame, as did Ramsey for his decision to take off Bobby Charlton.

Above: Holders Arsenal begin their 1971-72 Fairs Cup campaign with a trip to Lazio. The Gunners fell to Cologne in the quarters but had adequate compensation in winning the double.

DALGLISH TAKES OVER at NO. 7

Above: Liverpool's Kenny Dalglish beats Chelsea defender Micky Droy to the ball during a 1977-78 league match. It was the first taste of English football for Dalglish, a £440,000 close-season buy from Celtic. The man bought to take over Kevin Keegan's famous No. 7 shirt scored the goal which beat Bruges in that season's European Cup final. He went on to become the first man to score 100 goals north and south of the border.

Opposite: Dave Mackay leaps to join the celebratory scrum after Frank Saul puts Spurs 2-0 up in the 1967 Cup Final against Chelsea. A late Bobby Tambling goal was nothing more than a consolation for Chelsea; the first all-London final of the century was more one-sided than the 2-1 scoreline suggested.

ENGLAND'S FINEST HOUR

Opposite: Alf Ramsey's 1963 prediction of an England victory in the forthcoming World Cup comes to glorious fruition. Following the 4-2 win over West Germany, Ramsey believed that England would emulate the Hungarian side of the 1950s and set the new benchmark for all other international teams.

Right: Jimmy Greaves puts a congratulatory arm around the shoulder of Alan Ball as the victorious England team leave the Wembley pitch following their heroics in the World Cup final. Greaves was England's premier striker going into the competition, but he was out of touch in the opening group matches and a leg injury put him out of contention for the quarter-final clash with Argentina. Geoff Hurst stepped in to hit the only goal of the game, and Ramsey kept faith with the Hurst-Hunt partnership for the rest of the tournament. The decision surprised many but it was vindicated in the best possible way. Hurst's hat-trick in the final secured his place in football's hall of fame. It also answered those who feared that Ramsey's decision to dispense with wingers would blunt England's attack.

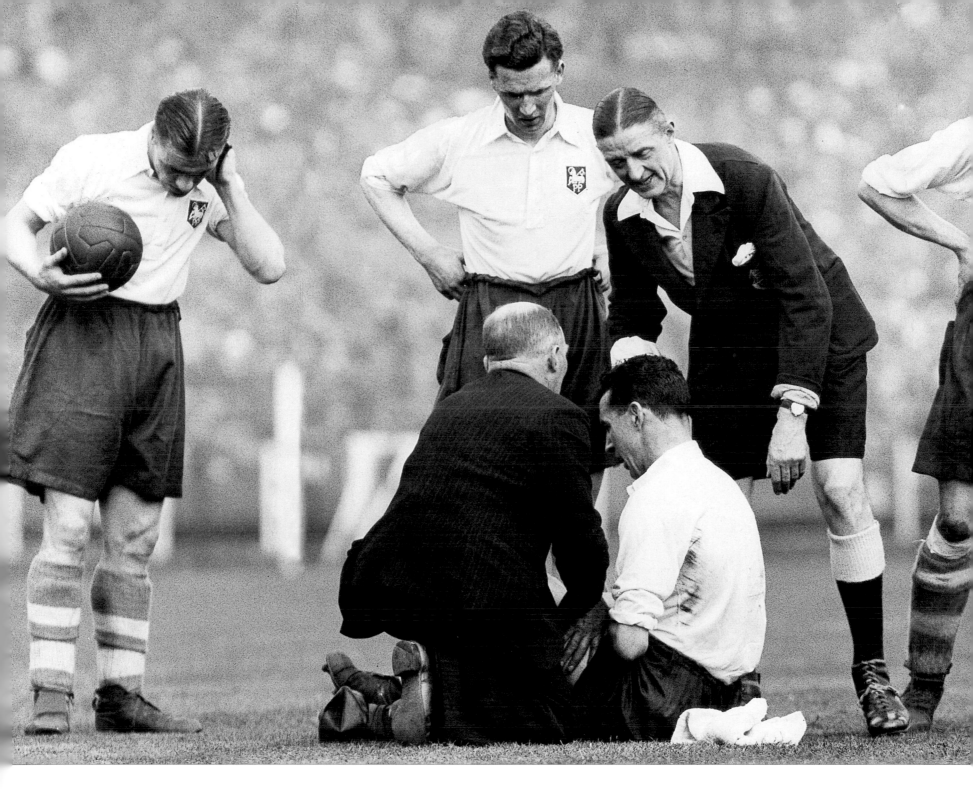

CUP JOY AT LAST FOR SUNDERLAND

Above: Preston North End centre-forward Frank O'Donnell receives treatment during the 1937 Cup Final. O'Donnell had put Preston 1-0 up against reigning champions Sunderland. The Rokermen had taken the 1935-36 title despite shipping a record 74 goals; 14 clubs had done better than that defensively. Sunderland were used to scoring more than they conceded, though, and in the 1937 final they struck three second-half goals to claim the club's first FA Cup success.

Opposite: Leicester manager Frank O'Farrell helps injured striker Allan Clarke off the field in their 1969 FA Cup semi-final against West Brom. Clarke had scored what proved to be the winner. At Wembley Leicester suffered their third defeat in nine years.

THE THEATRE OF DREAMS

Opposite: Bradford City and Newcastle fight out a goalless draw at Crystal Palace in the 1911 Cup Final. It was the Tynesiders' fifth appearance in the final in seven years, and not once did they manage a win at Crystal Palace. The replay venue this year was Old Trafford, which had been completed the previous year. That proved no happier hunting ground: Bradford won 1-0. Newcastle's only victory in this period was the replay at Goodison in 1910, where they beat Barnsley 2-1. The club has finished runners-up seven times in all, a record for the competition which they jointly hold with Arsenal and Everton.

Above: Arsenal team-mates Joe Mercer and Leslie Compton require treatment after clashing during a match against Blackpool in 1949. The Gunners won the league in 1947-48, Manchester United finishing runners-up. When the two met in Manchester that season it attracted a crowd of 83,260, a league record. The game took place at Maine Road, Old Trafford having suffered several direct hits during the war. The ground didn't open its gates again until August 1949; that must have pleased the board as well as the fans, since United had to pay City £5,000 for every game held there, plus a share of the gate receipts.

ONE VICTORY ENOUGH TO REACH FA CUP FINAL

Above: Making the draw for the most famous knockout competition in world football. Twelve clubs contested the first competition, in 1871. Wanderers had a walk-over in the first round, beat Clapham in the second, and reached the semis after drawing with Crystal Palace, the rules stating that in such an event both teams progressed. Their next opponents, Queens Park, also scratched, and Wanderers beat Royal Engineers in the final.

Opposite: Accrington Stanley captain Bob Wilson and the fixture that never was. Faced with mounting debts, Accrington, one of the 12 founder members of the Football League, had resigned four days earlier, their Fourth Division results expunged from the record. In 1883, 79 years earlier, the club had been expelled from the FA for paying players in the days of 'shamateurism'. The furore this and similar situations provoked caused the FA to relent and embrace professionalism in 1885.

FOOTBALL IS BACK

Opposite: Fans queuing to get into Ewood Park for a sixth-round replay between Blackburn and Huddersfield in the 1938-39 FA Cup. Huddersfield won 2-1; Blackburn had the consolation of finishing as Division Two champions, though it would be seven years before they could take their place back in the top flight.

Above: Stamford Bridge is packed to the rafters for the visit of Moscow Dynamo in November 1945. Chelsea fought out a 3-3 draw against a stylish Russian side who went on to beat Arsenal, the Gunners fielding several guest players as some of their squad were yet to be demobbed. The appetite for football as an antidote for six years of war was huge. There was no time to revive the league programme but the FA Cup returned, with matches up to the semi-finals played over two legs. The sixth-round meeting between Bolton and Stoke attracted a capacity crowd. Two crash barriers gave way in the crush and 33 people lost their lives.

SCOTS EXCEL IN THE PASSING GAME

Opposite: An aerial view of Hampden Park during the 1938 Scottish Cup Final. Either Rangers or Celtic had won all the previous finals that decade, but this year it was between East Fife and Kilmarnock, the former winning after a replay. Historically, Scottish teams had put the emphasis on team work and the passing game, whereas their southern counterparts, rooted in the public school system, tended to rely on

individual virtuosity. English clubs were quick to seek out the cream of Scottish talent; several players from north of the border starred for Preston's 'Invincibles', the team which remained undefeated in winning the inaugural league championship in 1888-89.

Above: A panoramic view of the 1914 Cup Final. After war broke out games sometimes took place behind closed doors so as not to disrupt armaments production.

GUNNERS LOOK TO EMULATE JAMES & CO.

Opposite: Highbury, August 1946. Three weeks before the return of league football George Male leads out a 'Probables' Arsenal XI against a team of promising youngsters. For all clubs it was a period of adjustment. Some of the stars of the prewar era would not return; all were seven years older. It did mean that clubs were keen to give talented young players their opportunity earlier than otherwise might have been the case. Hull City certainly did: that season 42 players turned out for the Third Division (North) side.

Left: Alex James leads out the Arsenal side which dominated English football in the 1930s. James was signed from Preston for £8,750 by Herbert Chapman after playing in the Scotland team which thrashed England 5-1 at Wembley in March 1928. James was a wayward genius, the Gascoigne of his day, someone who could create and finish with equal aplomb. It is said that when Germany came to play England at White Hart Lane in December 1935, a four-year-old supporter of the visitors knew only three English words: Arsenal, James and Bastin.

THE INCOMPARABLE GEORGE BEST

George Best shows his extraordinary balance and control as he leaves Chelsea defender Eddie MaCreadie on the deck (*above*), while the picture opposite shows that he was equally prodigious in aerial battles. Matt Busby said he had never seen a player who could beat an opponent in so many different ways. One of his team-mates once said that Best could have played in any outfield position for Manchester United and outperformed the usual incumbent, a remarkable claim for a side that included Law and Charlton, won the championship twice and were crowned kings of Europe in 1968. Best was dubbed the 'fifth Beatle' and had to deal with intense media scrutiny. There were footballing pressures too. By the end of the 1960s Best felt a new United team should have been moulded around him. After a number of spats, he walked out of Old Trafford for good in 1972, aged just 26.

HAIL THE CONQUERING HEROES

Above: Die-hard Gooners acclaim the 1950 Wembley victory over Liverpool. The Arsenal team included Compton brothers Denis and Leslie. The latter won his first England cap that year – at the age of 38. The Liverpool line-up included Joe Fagan, but another future manager, Bob Paisley, was left out of the side despite scoring in the semi-final win over Everton.

Opposite: 100,000 line the streets of Wolverhampton to welcome home their heroes after Wanderers' 3-1 defeat of Leicester City in the 1949 Cup Final. Leicester, who only just survived a Second Division relegation battle, gave a spirited display but couldn't recreate the form which had put out league champions Portsmouth in the semis. It was the start of a hugely successful era for Wolves, who were led on the field by Billy Wright and managed by his predecessor at the heart of the defence, Stan Cullis.

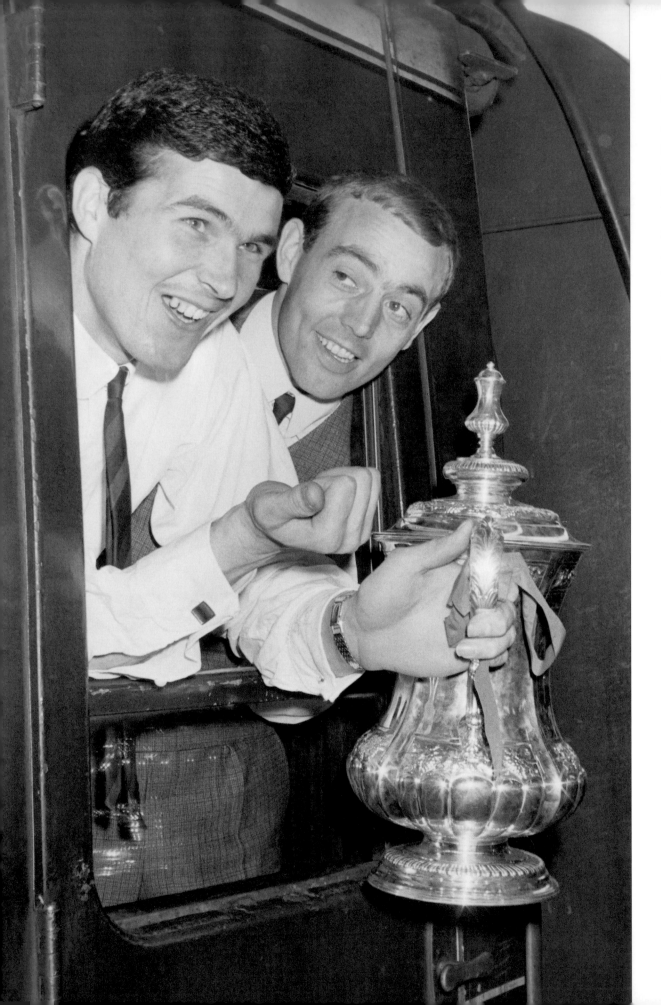

TRAUTMANN AND BYRNE SHRUG OFF WEMBLEY HOODOO

Opposite: Manchester City captain Roy Paul hands the Cup to goalkeeper Bert Trautmann during a celebratory dinner at the Cafe Royal. It was only after City's 3-1 win over Birmingham in the 1956 FA Cup Final that the seriousness of the neck injury he sustained during the match was revealed. Doctors said that it could easily have been fatal. Trautmann was the latest victim in a spate of Wembley injuries which became known as the 'Wembley hoodoo'. Some blamed the springiness of the turf for a number of serious leg injuries, which included fractures sustained by Nottingham Forest's Roy Dwight and Blackburn's Dave Whelan in 1959 and 1960 respectively.

Left: Ron Yeats and Ian St John keep their hands firmly on the Cup as they board the train to take it to Liverpool for the first time in the club's 73-year history. Five minutes into the 1965 final against Leeds, Gerry Byrne suffered a broken collar bone. With substitutes not permitted he played on through the pain barrier, and even set up the Reds' first goal, scored by Roger Hunt. Leeds levelled through Bremner but St John headed the winner in the second period of extra-time to give Liverpool the Cup in their third final appearance.

HONOURS EVEN IN BATTLE OF GIANTS

Above: A record crowd of 120,000 saw Aston Villa take on Sunderland at Crystal Palace in the 1913 Cup Final. This was double the previous year's gate, reflecting the fact that both sides were vying for the double. Barber scored the goal which won the Cup for Villa, but their title hopes faded when Sunderland got a vital point at Villa Park in their league encounter a few days later. Sunderland, who clinched the title

by beating Bolton, won 25 of their 38 games to finish with a record 54 points. As their first seven matches yielded just two draws, it was a truly remarkable performance.

Opposite: Thousands are locked out for this table-topping encounter between Arsenal and newly promoted Spurs in 1933-34. Herbert Chapman was a great publicist as well as manager: he negotiated the renaming of the local tube station from Gillespie Road to Arsenal.

159

CUP GOES OUT OF ENGLAND

Above: Sheffield United 'keeper Sutcliffe elects to punch clear during the 1925 Cup Final. Cardiff City, 1-0 losers that day, beat Arsenal two years later to take the FA Cup out of England for the first and only time. Gunners' Wales international 'keeper Dan Lewis allowed a Ferguson shot to slip through his grasp for the game's only goal. He later blamed the slippery sheen on his new jersey for the fumble. Cardiff weren't just a good cup side in the 1920s. In 1923-24 they went into their last league match at Birmingham a point clear of Huddersfield. Cardiff missed a penalty in their goalless draw, while Huddersfield won to bring them level on points. The Yorkshire club's goals column read 60-33, against Cardiff's 61-34, giving a fractionally superior goal average.

Opposite: Gordon Banks takes a comfortable catch during the 1966 World Cup final.

BEHIND EVERY GREAT TEAM...

Above: The 1965 Liverpool team pose with the FA Cup and Charity Shield. Bill Shankly's successor Bob Paisley (seated, right) would be far more successful in terms of silverware, and even Joe Fagan (standing, right) won the European Cup during his brief tenure in the manager's chair. But the Red revolution began with Shankly. Like all great managers, he was a great psychologist as well as being a first-rate coach and tactician. The famous 'This Is Anfield' sign over the entrance to the pitch was one of his ideas: it suggested a fortress and intimidated many more opponents than it inspired.

Opposite: Herbert Chapman (left), pictured with his Huddersfield Town team in 1921. Chapman turned an ailing club into league champions and FA Cup winners in just four years, then repeated the achievement with Arsenal. Chapman was years ahead of his time. While other teams were playing the old 2-3-5 system, Chapman introduced the much more fluid 'WM' formation. He championed floodlit matches, though these would not become commonplace until the 1950s, and also advocated the use of officials to adjudicate on goal-line controversies.

SCOTS CLAIM WORLD CHAMPIONSHIP

Opposite: Jimmy Greaves takes over in goal during an England training session in 1967, with the master, Gordon Banks, looking on. England had played just three games since their World Cup victory the previous year, beating Northern Ireland and Wales and drawing against Czechoslovakia. Next up were Scotland, in a European Championship qualifier. With Jim Baxter at his inspired best Scotland won the game 3-2, and their delirious

fans were quick to claim they were unofficial world champions. It was a short-lived moment of glory as the return fixture saw England get the draw they needed to progress to the last eight of the competition.
Above: West Ham goalkeeper Ernie Gregory manages to hang on to one of the balls fired at him during a training session prior to the 1952-53 season.

UNITED'S QUEST FOR EUROPEAN GLORY

Above: Manchester United players and staff get the feel of the Wembley turf prior to their European Cup Final against Benfica, 29 May 1968. Twelve years earlier the Football League had prevented Chelsea from entering the inaugural competition. Matt Busby was more far-sighted, immediately setting his sights on winning the trophy. United's first attempt, in 1956-57, was halted by holders Real Madrid at the semi-final stage. The following season AC Milan beat a team decimated by the Munich disaster. Partizan Belgrade ended their hopes in 1966; two years later United reached their first European final.

Opposite: United relish their Champions Cup triumph, gained from a 4-1 extra-time victory over the Portuguese giants. Munich survivors Charlton and Foulkes played in the match, the former hitting two of the goals. Busby had become the first manager to lead an English club side to European Cup glory.

IPSWICH SLIDE FOLLOWS DOUBLE CUP SUCCESS

Above: Bobby Robson and his players parade the FA Cup around Wembley after Ipswich's historic FA Cup win over Arsenal in 1978. It was the club's first appearance in the final in what was its centenary year. Three years later Ipswich won their first European trophy, beating Dutch side AZ 67 Alkmaar 5-4 on aggregate in the UEFA Cup Final. In 1982 Robson left Portman Road to take over the England job and Ipswich went on a steady slide, culminating in relegation in 1985-86. It brought to an end a 19-year run in the top flight, a record for the club.

Opposite: King George VI presents the Cup to Portsmouth skipper Jimmy Guthrie after Pompey's emphatic 4-1 win over hot favourites Wolves in 1939.

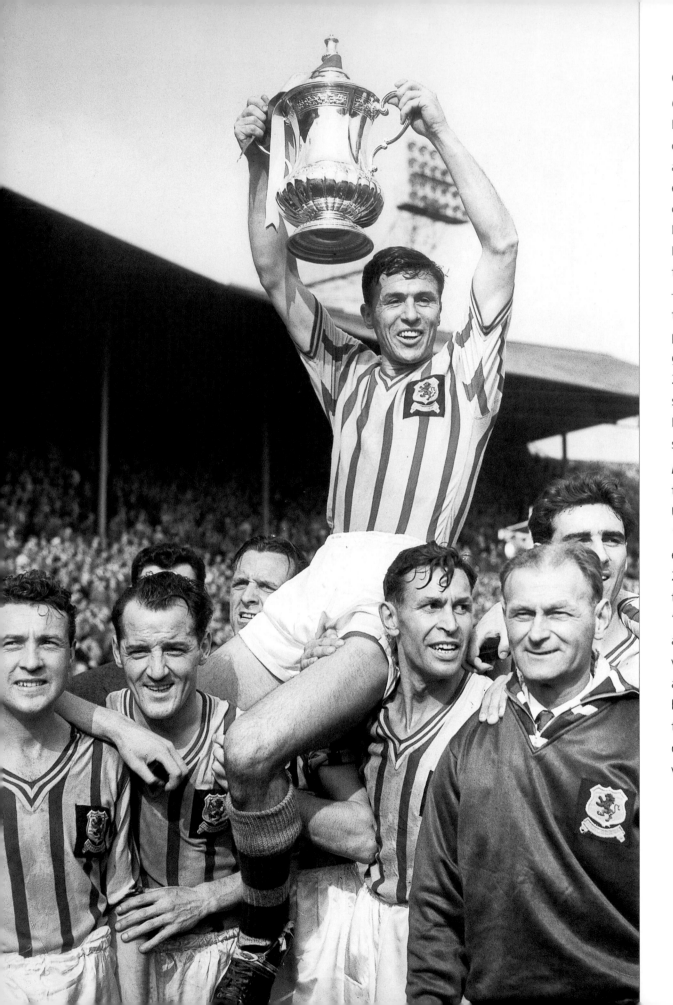

GUNNERS MATCH SPURS' ACHIEVEMENT

Opposite: Arsenal heroes Frank McLintock, Ray Kennedy and Charlie George celebrate completing the 1971 double, equalling the achievement of arch-rivals Spurs a decade earlier. The Gunners had wrapped up the championship with a 1-0 victory at White Hart Lane a few days earlier, the result consigning Leeds to the runners-up spot for the fourth time in seven years. Leeds lost just five games – one fewer than Arsenal – and their 64-point tally would have won the title in seven of the previous ten seasons. At Wembley extra-time goals from Eddie Kelly and George sealed a 2-1 victory over Liverpool. It was a particularly sweet moment for Footballer of the Year McLintock, who had finished on the losing side with Leicester three times in the 1960s.

Left: Aston Villa captain Johnny Dixon hoists the Cup aloft after his side dash Manchester United's hopes of winning the double in 1956-57. United romped to the league title, eight points clear of their nearest rivals and 21 ahead of mid-table Villa. The match turned on yet another Wembley injury, United 'keeper Ray Wood fracturing a cheekbone in a clash with Peter McParland when the game was just six minutes old. Jackie Blanchflower acquitted himself well as the stand-in 'keeper but brave United went down 2-1. It meant that Villa remained the last club to do the double, in 1896-97, although that record would stand for just four more years.

INJURED PUSKAS BRINGS WORLD CUP AGONY FOR HUNGARY

Above: Puskas (left) and Hidas, two of Hungary's all-star team of the 1950s, in relaxed mood before beating Scotland 4-2 at Hampden Park on 8 December 1954. The team's only reverse in four years had come six months earlier, in the World Cup final. West Germany coach Sepp Herberger played an understrength team against Hungary in the group stage and lost 8-3. They met again in the final, and with Puskas carrying an injury the Germans pulled off a famous 3-2 victory.

Opposite: Jimmy Greaves and Danny Blanchflower prepare for Spurs' 1962 European Cup semi-final clash with Benfica. They narrowly failed to turn round a 3-1 deficit from the away leg.

SPURS MATCH GUNNERS' RECORD

Opposite: With Dave Mackay as usual in the thick of the action, Spurs wheel away to acclaim yet another goal. On this occasion an inswinging corner from mercurial winger John White needed no assistance from any of the Spurs' attackers. Spurs scored 115 goals en route to the 1960-61 championship, equalling Arsenal's feat of 1934-35. The avalanche brought them a record 31 wins, 16 of them on their travels. Their 66-point haul matched the Gunners' achievement of 1930-31. Spurs failed to reach the same heights after the break-up of their double-winning side, which included the tragic death of White. The man nicknamed 'The Ghost' was killed by lightning while playing golf in 1964.

Above: Everton score against Spurs at a muddy White Hart Lane in 1954.

THE PHYSICAL BATTLE

Above: Joe Jordan (left) and Dave Watson had many bruising battles for club and country in the 1970s. Jordan made his name with Leeds, where he spent seven years before moving to Old Trafford in 1978. Capped 52 times for Scotland, Jordan got on the scoresheet in three successive World Cups (1974-82); no other Scot has achieved that feat. Watson was a rock at the heart of the Sunderland defence in the 1973 FA Cup victory. A move to Manchester City followed, and he went on to win 65 England caps between 1974 and 1982.

Opposite: A close shave for Whitworth, the Leicester City full back, as Arsenal's Charlie George rushes towards goal with a foot held high at Highbury in September 1973.

AULD ENEMY INFLICT WORST EVER DEFEAT

Opposite: Wembley, 15 April 1961. Scotland's goalkeeper Frank Haffey watches in despair as a seventh England goal hits the back of his net. The match against the 'auld enemy' ended in a 9-3 rout, Scotland's heaviest defeat in 91 years of international football. Greaves hit a hat-trick, Bobby Smith and Johnny Haynes a brace each, with Bobby Robson and Bryan Douglas also joining the party. Earlier that season England had put five

goals past both Wales and Northern Ireland to win the home international championship at a canter, but a year later a lacklustre team disappointed at the World Cup in Chile.

Above: West Bromwich Albion heading for a 3-2 victory over Preston North End in the 1954 Cup Final.

MORTENSEN PULLS ON WALES' SHIRT

Opposite: Wembley, 19 January 1946. England captain Joe Mercer introduces Stanley Matthews to Prime Minister Clement Attlee before the team's match against Belgium. This was one of five Victory internationals played in the year following the end of hostilities. England won three of them, including a 2-0 win over the Belgians. Like the wartime internationals, these were not counted as part of the official record. One

reason for this was the much more relaxed approach to the rules that pertained during this period. In one England v Wales match in 1943 Stan Mortensen turned out for the opposition. England still ran out 8-3 winners.
Above: The Duke of Edinburgh shakes hands with Matthews before the 1953 FA Cup Final between Blackpool and Bolton. After two Wembley defeats in five years, Matthews made this final his own.

NICHOLSON ENDS GREAVES' ITALIAN NIGHTMARE

Above: Jimmy Greaves opens his account on his debut for Chelsea – against the team with whom he would enjoy his most prolific spell. Greaves scored first time out for every team he played for, including England, although on the latter occasion it was a consolation goal in a 4-1 defeat against Peru in May 1959. Greaves signed off from Stamford Bridge at the age of 21 with 41 league goals in 1960-61; that made him the First Division's top marksman for the second time in three years. Spurs boss Bill Nicholson rescued him from a brief unhappy spell at AC Milan, paying the Italians £99,999 so as not to burden the striker with the tag of being the first £100,000 player.

Opposite: Greaves adds to his England tally in the 4-2 win over Spain at Wembley in October 1960.

BRINGING THE HOUSE DOWN

Above: Scotland fans invade the pitch after their team's historic 3-2 win over the world champions at Wembley in April 1967. For many this match exorcised the pain of the 9-3 defeat six years earlier and warranted a memento: sections of the Wembley turf were soon on their way north of the border.

Opposite: Wolves' captain Billy Wright (far right) considers the options after the goal collapses in their game against Bournemouth.

'BANKS OF ENGLAND'

Left: 'Banks of England' was a fitting nickname for arguably the country's greatest ever goalkeeper. Gordon Banks was England's first choice between the posts for a decade, despite the fact that he didn't play for one of the glamour clubs. He began his career with Chesterfield, joining Leicester City in 1959. He was twice an FA Cup runner-up with the Foxes, though he did pick up a League Cup winners' medal in 1964. In 1967 Banks moved to Stoke, a mediocre First Division side. His five years at the Victoria Ground produced another League Cup victory, a modest return in the domestic game for an outstanding 18-year career. On the international front it was a different matter entirely, Banks kept a remarkable 35 clean sheets in his 73 appearances for England. Ironically, it is for two games in which he conceded that he is best remembered: the 4-2 victory over West Germany in the 1966 World Cup final; and the brilliant diving save to keep out a powerful Pele header in Mexico four years later. He won the Footballer of the Year award in 1972, the year in which the loss of an eye in a road accident ended his career in top-flight football.

Opposite: 1952 FA Cup Final. Arsenal 'keeper George Swindin makes a clean catch with Newcastle forwards Jackie Milburn and George Robledo in close attendance. Robledo scored the only goal of the game, making Newcastle the first 20th century club to retain the trophy.

THERE ARE PEOPLE ON THE PITCH...

Above: Chelsea fans try to take the law into their own hands after a bad tackle on one of their own by an Everton player. Pitch invasions became a constant blight on the British game, even when there was no malicious intent. During the 1966 FA Cup Final an Everton fan treated TV audiences to one of the finest chases ever seen on that medium. That same year the most famous piece of commentary of all time described fans whose eagerness to join the celebrations overstepped the mark. The height of perimeter fencing was sometimes increased to combat the problem, though things never quite reached the scale of South America, where eight-feet-deep moats were not unheard of. The tragedies at Heysel, Hillsborough and Bradford in the 1980s brought home the risk of penning in fans too rigidly.

Opposite: Millwall and Manchester City fans leave the pitch swiftly to evade celebrating fans.

VICTORY OVER WORLD CHAMPIONS MASKS SLOW DECLINE

Above: Walter Winterbottom gives his England side a team talk in preparation for a game against Wales at Wembley on 10 November 1954. England won 3-2, and a month later scored a 3-1 victory over newly crowned world champions West Germany. Such results masked a steady decline in England's fortunes and its standing in the world game. Training sessions in the Winterbottom era were undemanding, organisation often bordered on the farcical. At a function almost two decades after England

conceded 13 goals in two games to the Hungarians, Puskas overheard full-backs Alf Ramsey and Bill Eckersley tentatively reacquainting themselves. Puskas remarked that in those two memorable matches the England players barely seemed to know each other.

Opposite: Matt Busby gives his Manchester United players an impromptu team talk.

MERCER JOINS EXCLUSIVE CLUB

Above: Manchester City warming up for the 1969 FA Cup Final in the red-and-black striped shirts they would wear at Wembley. Neil Young scored the goal which beat Leicester City, giving the blue half of Manchester their fourth – and most recent – success in the competition. Captain Tony Book was named joint Footballer of the Year, along with Derby's Dave Mackay. City briefly challenged the likes of neighbours United, Liverpool, Leeds and Everton for domestic supremacy. Joe Mercer's men had won the championship the year before, and added both the League Cup and Cup-Winners' Cup to the trophy cabinet in

1970. City's 1967-68 league title meant that Mercer joined Ted Drake, Bill Nicholson and Alf Ramsey as the only men to have won the championship as both player and manager.

Opposite: George Best and Mike Summerbee, legends on the red and blue sides of the Mancunian divide, were good friends off the pitch and even went into the retail fashion business together. Best's days at the top coincided with a fallow period for Northern Ireland. Summerbee won just eight England caps between 1968 and 1973, scoring once.

CARTER LEADS SUNDERLAND TO FIRST FA CUP

Above: Bobby Gurney equalises for Sunderland against Preston in the 1937 FA Cup Final. The Rokermen came back from a 1-0 half-time deficit to win 3-1. The scorer of the second goal was Horatio 'Raich' Carter, one of the all-time great inside-forwards. His 213 league goals came at almost one every two games, and he bettered that strike rate for England, hitting

7 in 13 appearances. Although his career spanned the Second World War – he won the FA Cup again with Derby in 1946 – his record would undoubtedly have been even greater but for that seven-year hiatus.

Opposite: Goalmouth action from the 1933 Cup Final between Everton and Manchester City, the first in which numbered shirts were used.

CHIVERS JOINS SPURS IN RECORD DEAL

Above: Martin Chivers, who joined Spurs from Southampton for a British record £125,000 in 1968. Chivers hit both goals in the League Cup final victory over Aston Villa in 1971, and a year later his brace helped Spurs to a 3-2 aggregate win over Wolves in the inaugural UEFA Cup Final. He scored 13 goals in 24 appearances for England. In many of those games the forward line comprised the '3 Cs', Mick Channon and Allan Clarke making up the triumvirate.

Opposite: Chivers in an aerial duel with the Chelsea defence.

CUP FINAL MOVED TO AVOID BOAT RACE CLASH

Opposite: Huddersfield on the attack against Aston Villa in the 1920 Cup Final. Villa won the match 1-0 for a record sixth success in the competiton. 72,000 people packed into Stamford Bridge that day; the Cup Final had come a long way since 1873, when the showpiece of the footballing calendar was held in the morning to avoid clashing with the prestigious Boat Race.

Above: Action from the Huddersfield-Preston Cup Final of 1922, the first to be decided by a penalty. Huddersfield's Billy Smith scored what was the game's only goal.

CHARLTONS CLOCK UP 1200 GAMES IN 40 YEARS

Opposite: 1973 marked the end of an era for Manchester United and Leeds United. Bobby Charlton left to join Preston, ending a 20-year association with Old Trafford. Jack had managerial spells at Middlesbrough, Sheffield Wednesday and Newcastle, and took the

Republic of Ireland to successive World Cup finals in 1990 and 1994. The Charlton brothers hold the appearance record for their respective clubs, both having played over 600 league matches.

Above: North London rivalries are put aside as Spurs' Terry Venables does the best-man honours for Arsenal's George Graham.

GOLDEN ERA FOR BEES

Above: The Arsenal-Brentford fixture on Good Friday of the 1937-38 season was almost a top-of-the-table clash. The Bees had risen from the Third Division (South) to the top flight in four years. This would be the club's third successive top-six finish, though the slide back whence they came began the next season. Meanwhile, the Gunners claimed their fifth championship in eight years.

Opposite: Charlton on their way to a 2-0 win over Bolton in the semi-final of the 1945-46 FA Cup. In the final Bert Turner became the first man to score at both ends. Charlton lost 4-1 to Derby.

REDS ENDURE TWO-WEEK WAIT TO CLAIM TITLE

Opposite: Having lost in the first postwar Cup Final, Charlton made it to Wembley again in 1947. A Chris Duffy volley gave the Addicks a 1-0 win over Burnley. League football returned this year, the winter freeze causing the season to be extended to June. Liverpool were top having completed their programme but had an anxious two-week wait as Stoke could have pipped them by beating Sheffield United. Stoke lost and the Reds took their fifth title.

Above: A packed Highbury watches the team of the 1930s. Between 1931 and 1939 the Gunners finished no lower than sixth.

IPSWICH COMPLETE PROMOTION-CHAMPIONSHIP DOUBLE

Above: Ipswich fans flock to Portman Road during the run-in to the team's 1960-61 Second Division campaign. A Third Division (South) side just four years earlier, Alf Ramsey's men won promotion to the top flight for the first time in the club's history, then lifted the championship at the first attempt. Only Liverpool (1905-6), Everton (1931-2) and Spurs (1950-1) had managed that feat. Ramsey added just one player to his promotion-winning squad.

Opposite: A crowd of 133,000 at Hampden Park to watch England's 3-2 win over Scotland in a 1944 wartime international.

COUNTDOWN TO THE FINAL FOR WORLD CUP STARS

Above: England players take a leisurely stroll three days before the 1966 World Cup final, (l-r) Ron Springett, Peter Bonetti, Nobby Stiles and Alan Ball. With Gordon Banks in imperious form, neither of the second-string 'keepers was required. Stiles provided bite and protection as the midfield holding player, while 21-year-old Ball had one of the key roles in Ramsey's new system, playing as a withdrawn winger. It was one of his many raids down the flanks that created the opportunity for England's controversial third goal, scored by Hurst.

Opposite: Arsenal's Eddie Hapgood, Frank Moss and Alex James admire the burgeoning skills of James' son Tony.

SPURS BREAK BRITAIN'S DUCK IN EUROPE

Above and opposite: Gala celebrations as Tottenham become the first British club to lift a European trophy. Spurs had gone out to Benfica in the European Cup semi-final in 1961-62 and slipped to third in the league. But Bill Nicholson's side retained the FA Cup to give them a second crack at European competition in 1962-63. The team eased past Glasgow Rangers, Slovan Bratislava and OFK Belgrade, setting up a final against holders Atletico Madrid. Spurs brushed aside the loss of Dave Mackay through injury to take a 2-0 lead. Atletico pulled one back from the spot, but with a second goal from Greaves and two from Terry Dyson Spurs were emphatic 5-1 winners.

TO [T]NHAM HOTSPUR F.C.
EUROPEAN CUP WINNERS CUP ~
WINNERS 1963

NEW BOY TAYLOR SINKS FULHAM

Opposite: Trevor Brooking is mobbed by Hammers fans after the team's 2-0 win over Second Division side Fulham in the 1975 FA Cup final. It was a year when nearly all the big guns went out early: of the top six in the league only Ipswich made it to the last eight. West Ham accounted for Bobby Robson's side in the semis, Alan Taylor hitting both goals in a

2-1 replay victory after the first meeting ended goalless. Taylor, in his first season at Upton Park, went on to score the two Wembley goals which sank Bobby Moore's Fulham.

Above: Blackpool's 1953 Cup-winning side make a guest appearance on the popular TV show *What's My Line?*

OLD TRAFFORD SUFFERS DIRECT HIT

Opposite: Clearing up begins at Old Trafford, whose main stand took a direct hit during the Second World War. After the conflict United received a £22,000 grant from the War Damage Commission to effect repairs. The rebuilt stadium was finally ready at the start of the 1949-50 campaign.

Above: Umbrellas are the order of the day at the 1925 Cup Final. The 'People's Game' has had many peaks and troughs, though even at its lowest points no other sport has challenged its pre-eminent position in the sporting calendar. In 1948-49 over 40 million people went through the turnstiles to watch their team.

'MY RIGHT-HAND MAN'

Right: Alf Ramsey confers with Bobby Moore, the player he would call 'my right-hand man, my lieutenant in the field'. One of Ramsey's first acts when he took over from Walter Winterbottom in 1963 was to make Moore captain, the youngest Englishman ever to lead his country onto the pitch. Moore had no great pace and was indifferent in the air, yet Pele would regard him as the world's greatest defender. His reading of the game was second to none, his timing and passing impeccable. When he bowed out of football in 1973 Moore had won 108 caps, breaking Bobby Charlton's record. Since then only Peter Shilton has pulled on an international jersey more times; Moore thus remains England's most capped outfield player. He died from bowel cancer in 1993, aged 51.

Left: England's Johnny Haynes, Bobby Smith and Jimmy Greaves. Greaves' 44 goals from 57 games was a phenomenal return, yet in the early 1960s his Spurs team-mate Bobby Smith more than matched him, hitting the net 13 times in his 15 England outings. He also scored in both of Tottenham's Cup Final victories of 1961 and 1962. Haynes' record of 18 goals in 56 games was also impressive for a midfielder.

UNLIKELY HEROES

Above: Sunderland players celebrate in the bath following their FA Cup semi-final victory in 1973. Bob Stokoe's team went on to achieve a famous victory over Leeds United in the final with Ian Porterfield scoring the winning goal.

Opposite: Aston Villa players weighing-in after reporting back for pre-season training in 1956.

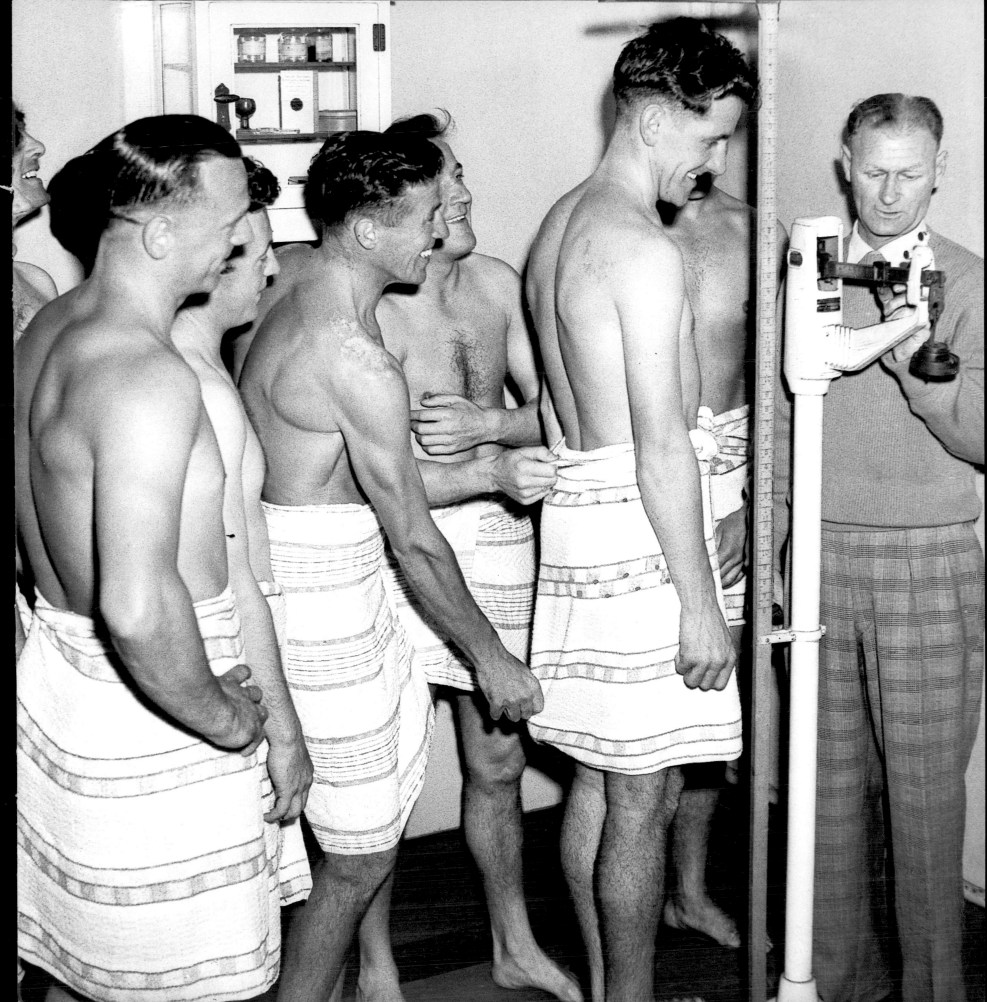

IRON MAN MACKAY BRUSHES ASIDE DOUBLE LEG BREAK

Left: Spurs' skipper Dave Mackay and Alan Mullery celebrate the club's 2-1 Cup Final win over Chelsea in 1967, their third victory in seven years. Mackay was one of the most influential players of his era, the archetypal midfield driving force. His appearance in the 1967 Wembley final was a testament to his indomitable spirit and iron constitution, for three years earlier he broke his left leg twice inside a 12-month period. Not only did he recover to captain Spurs to further Cup glory but in 1969 he won the Footballer of the Year award. By then he was a Derby player, and he had just guided the Rams to the Second Division championship. Mackay went on to manage Derby, taking over from Brian Clough in 1974. A year later he emulated Clough's 1972 achievement in bringing the championship to the Baseball Ground. Mackay thus became only the fifth man to win the league as both player and manager.

Opposite: Johnny Carey is chaired off the field following Manchester United's 4-2 win over Blackpool in the 1948 Cup Final. United reached their first final in nearly 40 years the hard way, meeting First Division opposition in every round. They twice came from behind to make Blackpool their sixth scalp from the top flight, a record for the competition. It was the first piece of silverware of the Matt Busby era.